Enda
THE WAY HOME

"In *The Way Home*, Lindsey very methodically gives you chapter by chapter , the trap that deception played in driving her away from her home. Someone who was so anointed, creative, loved and revered, just like that, was caught in a web of deception that she had no idea how to get out of except, for the love of the Father, family and a faithful husband. Lindsey very passionately lays out God's plan for a healed and restored marriage, when it seemed all hope was gone. This is a story of restoration, recovery, and a bona fide MIRACLE! If you are in, feel like you are going to be in, know someone who right now is in, a situation that a marriage is ending, about to end, or has ended, Lindsey throws out the rope of hope. This girl made it back home and you can too. I know God hears and answers prayer, this book is proof! Read it and find the Way Home."

Jamie and Judy Jacobs Tuttle
His Song Ministries, Dwelling Place Church International

"*The Way Home* is honest, brave and sincere. We believe it will touch so many hearts—the one who feels so lost without hope . . . the spouse that prays to understand the "why" behind their husband or wives struggles . . . the parent praying for a child running the wrong path . . . anyone in need of encouragement to keep on believing. Lindsey has been through the fire, fought her way out, and now she is a guide and friend leading us toward courage in out personal battles. We have faced similar adversity in our own marriage. Lindsey and her husband Casey have been a beacon of light and hope in our own dark times. We are forever grateful for their transparency and willingness to embrace us, share their story and their hearts, reminding us that we are not alone."

Kevin and Krista McBride

"I remember being in a Wednesday night service at the Ramp, in September 2015, while I was speaking my heart was broken for Casey as he sat on the front row, on the edge of a certain divorce. I felt the Lord tell me to sing over him the old chorus line, "God will make a way where there seems to be no way." So I did, even though at that point it looked like his marriage was totally over, with no possible way back. Then, in January of 2016, I got a call out telling me that Casey and Lindsey were back together and head over heals in love. This was nothing short of a miracle. God indeed had powerfully worked behind the scenes of what looked impossible and had made a way. This book is the very honest account of how He did it, so buckle in for a heart-stirring, shocking, eye-opening and totally amazing ride. We rejoice with you, Casey and Lindsey, this book is your true story. Thank you for sharing it with the world. It's a story of the power of redemption and of redemptive love that needs to be heard. We love you both dearly and cheer you on as God leads you into new adventures, hand in hand."

Andy and Gina Elmes
Senior Pastors, Family Church, Portsmouth, UK

"This is a book of hope. Raw and real, Lindsey steps out of hiding and exposes the enemy that deceived her and the God that came to her rescue. It is a beautiful story of love and restoration. It gives renewed faith to every father and mother believing for the return of sons and daughters. It gives direction to those who have lost their way and want to find the way home."

Karen Wheaton
The Ramp, Hamilton, AL

The WAY HOME

Hope is not lost!

The WAY HOME

LINDSEY DOSS

© Copyright 2017 Lindsey Doss

This edition published in 2017 by Great Big Life Publishing
Empower Centre, 83-87 Kingston Road, Portsmouth, PO2 7DX, UK.

The right of Lindsey Doss to be identified as the authors of this work has been
asserted by them in accordance with the Copyright, Designs and Patents Act
1988. All rights reserved. No part of this publication may be reproduced or
transmitted in any form or by any means, electronic or mechanical, including
photocopy, recording or any information storage and retrieval system, without
permission in writing from the publisher.

British Library Cataloguing in Publication Data. A catalogue record for this book
is available from the British Library

Unless otherwise marked, Scripture quotations are taken from Holy Bible, New
Living Translation, copyright © 1996, 2004, 2015 by Tyndale House Foundation.
Used by permission of Tyndale House Publishers Inc., Carol Stream, Illinois
60188. All rights reserved.

Scripture quotations marked 'NKJV' are taken from New King James Version®,
copyright © 1982 by Thomas Nelson. Used by permission. All rights reserved.

Scripture quotations marked 'AMP' are taken from The Amplified Bible, copyright
© 2015 by The Lockman Foundation, La Habra, CA 90631. All rights reserved.

Scripture quotations marked 'The Message' (MSG) are taken from The Message,
copyright © 1993, 1994, 1995, 1996, 2000, 2001, 2002. Used by permission of
NavPress Publishing Group.

ISBN-13: 978-0-9957925-6-2
ISBN-10: 0995792569
eBook ISBN: 978-0-9957925-7-9

CONTENTS

DEDICATION

Analeise, Katie, and Asher:
You're the most treasured part of my life and I'm honored
to be your mommy.

Casey:
"And I'd choose you; in a hundred lifetimes, in a hundred
worlds, in any version of reality, I'd find you and I'd
choose you." The Chaos of Stars
I love you forever

FOREWORD

My life from 2011 to 2016 was pure hell. A storm hit our home that I never saw coming. After years of trying to put my finger on exactly what was happening in my marriage, with the aid of countless counselors, I was still at a loss. None of the advice or formulas I was applying were generating the results they were supposed to. All the "words" and "promises" people gave me were not coming to pass and the faith teaching I had grown up on and even preached to others still left me without the outcomes I so desperately wanted. Although the word 'divorce' was never spoken in our home, I had no idea its reality was actually boiling below the surface.

Once Lindsey actually left and I was handed the divorce papers, I was totally discombobulated. I never in a million years thought I would find myself in such a place. That event set in motion the most painful eighteen months of my life. After ministering for years to others, I felt quite certain I knew what hurt was.

I had no clue.

However, that experience also taught me something else. As cliche as it sounds, I had a front-row seat to the greatest miracle I've ever witnessed. Simply put, nothing is too hard for God.

I wish I could write this Foreword about some great test of faith I had mastered and how I stood fast, hoping against hope, believing beyond belief, never wavering, and knowing all along what the outcome of the situation was going to be.

And I did do all of those things, it just depended on which day you caught me on, because those faith-filled moments were also laced with days full of doubt, days where I just wanted the pain to stop, for closure to come so I could pick up the pieces and start over again. The times I believed God for Lindsey to come home at any moment were counter-balanced by times of thinking I would never get to hug or kiss my wife ever again, I'd never get to hold her hand, see a movie with her, or sit on the sand and watch our kids playing in the ocean together.

People ask me often about that season. I'm still not able to talk about it too much. It ran deep—real deep. But for those of you who might be in my situation, I have a few thoughts that perhaps might help you. Some were advice given to me by the amazing leaders in my life who were always a phone call away to help guide or to just listen. Others are things I learned on my own.

First, give yourself permission to be wherever you are at. If you are full of faith then great, keep going. If you are fighting doubt, I feel you. I've been there. Don't condemn yourself when you feel more like Chicken Little than Smith Wigglesworth.

Second, don't grow bitter toward those causing the pain and heartbreak—no matter what they do. Keep your heart clean from it. I know it's hard, but you have to.

Third, it is absolutely crucial that you surround yourself with people who will love and support you. For me, it was a handful of friends that would come by on Wednesday nights after church and just hang out with me. Sometimes we would talk about the divorce; sometimes it would never be mentioned. I will be eternally grateful to Jason, Winfred, Mike, and Richard who were always there. They were true friends, and also my chess victims.

Fourth, for those of you who are married, when you don't have love to draw from, then simply draw from the fact you made a covenant. Even if they have broken theirs, you keep yours. God will reward you for it in the end. Fight to keep your heart open to restoration until God says otherwise—and you will know if He does. If you think He almost, might have, could have, released you but you're not sure . . . then He hasn't. Keep fighting.

Lastly, again for those who are married, guard your mind against other relationships. Don't go there even on an emotional or thought level. If you do, you probably won't be able to come back.

I wish I could tell you with certainty that your prodigal will come home. But I won't. Only God has the answer.

But can they? Can He really reach your loved one who has become a different person right in front of your very eyes? Can He actually change and transform them after everything they have done, after all the lines they have crossed, after they have said and done things you never dreamed they would do?

Absolutely.

Casey Doss

Chapter 1

CAUTION

*"But then I will win her back once again. I will
lead her into the desert and speak tenderly to her
there. I will return her vineyards to her and transform
the Valley of Trouble into a gateway of hope. She will
give herself to me there, as she did long ago when she
was young, when I freed her from her captivity in Egypt.
When that day comes", says the LORD, "you will call
me 'my husband' instead of 'my master.' . . . I will
make you my wife forever, showing you righteousness
and justice, unfailing love and compassion."*
Hosea 2:14-16, 19

I have a tale to tell. A tale of a girl who once was, and
the journey she took to find her way back home. There
was only one problem . . . she had destroyed her home.
Stories of restored marriages are usually told from the pen
of the conquering hero. But this time is different. This

story is being told from the heart of the villain. The story you are about to read is true, for I was that villain. I was the one who left home and had to try and find my way back.

I was raised in church my entire life. My family has faithfully served God for many generations. My mother was a world-renowned gospel singer who had ministered to hundreds of thousands of people. However, despite the godly upbringing I had, as I grew older, got married, and had children, I found myself at a personal crossroads. One path led to truth, while the other led to destruction. Once I finally faced this deep conflict within myself, I decided to run as fast and hard as I could down a road that I *thought* would lead one way, but turned out to lead me someplace radically different.

My decisions hurt people in horrific ways. I destroyed lives. I drove others down the road of destruction along with me. Some have still not found their way back, and their blood is on my hands. My repentance also inspired others. I became the one who did the difficult thing when all hope seemed lost.

Of all the ways the enemy was at work in my life, deception was his most prominent weapon. This book paints a picture of what happens when you not only believe the lie of the enemy, but you act on it. It is an illustration of what living a life of deception costs. There is an old song called *The Snake* written by Al Wilson. The lyrics are frighteningly accurate in how the enemy paints a beautiful picture for us, wears a beautiful mask, and then destroys us. Before we begin our story, I want us to carefully consider these lyrics:

On her way to work one morning
Down the path along side the lake
A tender-hearted woman saw a poor half-frozen snake
His pretty colored skin had been all frosted with the dew
"Poor thing," she cried, "I'll take you in and I'll take care of you."
"Take me in, oh tender woman
Take me in, for heaven's sake
Take me in, oh tender woman," sighed the snake.

She wrapped him up all cozy in a comforter of silk
And laid him by her fireside with some honey and some milk.
She hurried home from work that night and soon as she arrived
She found that pretty snake she'd taken to, had been revived.
"Take me in, oh tender woman
Take me in, for heaven's sake
Take me in, oh tender woman," sighed the snake.

She clutched him to her bosom, "You're so beautiful,"
she cried
"If I hadn't brought you in by now you might have
died."
Now she stroked his pretty skin and then she kissed and
held him tight
But instead of saying thanks, that snake gave her a
vicious bite.

"I saved you!" cried the woman
"And you've bitten me even, why?!
You knew your bite is poison and now I'm going to die."
"Oh shut up, silly woman," said the reptile with a grin,
"You knew good and well I was a snake before you took
me in." [1]

How dangerous deception is! How much it can destroy!
Just like in the song, deception paints itself in the most
beautiful of colors! And it is different for each person.
"Beauty is in the eye of the beholder." We have all heard
this phrase, and deception works in the exact same way.
What seems beautiful to me may not be beautiful to you.
What is beautiful to you may not be beautiful to me. But
deception can paint itself in any color. It can take on
any appearance. It comes in the form of everything you
have ever wanted, and it comes at a time you are already

---

1   *The Snake*, Al Wilson

weak. What a dangerous thing deception is! What a tool the enemy has in using deception . . . but there is hope. We, as believers, have been given everything we need to defeat this horrible, deceitful, venomous snake. We need only to reach out and take it. You may not know when you are deceived, but you know when you are not.

For me, deception was merely the first step to my radical lifestyle change. Before I knew what was happening, I was drowning in fear, shame, guilt, and sin . . . and I never saw it coming. I became another person completely. I lost sight of what I wanted and who I was.

When traveling, if you make a wrong turn it is easy to turn around or simply allow the sat-nav to "reroute" you. Unfortunately for me, I ended up down a road I was almost unable to come back from. I never knew my choices would cost me so much. I never knew I would hurt so many people. I never knew I would have so much blood on my hands. What do you do when you are so lost that all you want to hear is "Proceed to the route", but when you look around there is no route to be seen? There is nothing. You can't even find the road. Now, the only option is to start all over with your directions in hope that you may be able to get back to where you wanted to go.

Within this book you will find both my story and the lessons I learned along my journey. Each is important and carries crucial lessons. My hope is that you catch a glimpse into the mind of a deceived woman and the choices that almost cost her everything. I also want to reveal the one decision that changed my life forever. I hope to reach people like me who were lost, and people like you who are believing for someone else to come home. If you are the latter, allow my story to give you a glimpse into the thoughts of a prodigal. I pray you find yourself in both the sorrows and triumphs of these pages. As you take this journey back in time with me, understand there were many people involved with my choices. And for the sake of privacy, some of their names and identities have been changed in this book.

Now . . . let us begin the journey home together.

Chapter 2

IT IS FINISHED

We had a happy home, once. He loved me. I loved him. Many people pat me on the back and say, "It will turn out all right in the end." But little do they know, I was the one who landed my husband and me in the side room of a courthouse, and I had done it for a good reason; or so I thought. It's certainly not the first time I've been wrong.

So many things have contributed to this moment that I couldn't pinpoint any one specific thing that cost me my marriage. Most divorces are final after six months. But for us, this has been two years of pure hell. I think I remember calling off one of our mediations in order to work on repairing our relationship, but I don't remember now for certain. And it really wouldn't even matter if I did. I'm too far gone, and we are far, far, far from hope.

It is late fall of 2015. We've been here for hours and my head is pounding as I listen to Dianne, my attorney, negotiate custody arrangements with the mediator. I hear the text alert on my phone.

"Everything going ok, sweetie? Haven't heard from you in a couple of hours," my dad says. After my own parents' divorce it was my grandfather, Papaw Bill, who really took on the father role. But after the stroke that claimed his life, I had no one. Right now is the first time in my life my father Scott and I have ever been close. My mother had custody of my sister and me, and we saw him on occasional weekends. He never really pulled in to us or made any effort to be close, but now, oddly, he and his wife Joyce are the only two people who have really supported me through my divorce. It is what I have always wanted since I was a little girl, to be close to and be loved by my daddy. I hate how I have lied to them about why the divorce is happening though, especially considering all they have done to help me get through it. I didn't lie intentionally, of course—I was believing my own lies at the time, but still, I was the one who started spreading the bitter poison of offense. We would all sit around gossiping about and slandering all the people who had taken Casey's side of our divorce, especially my own family, adding more and more offense until, between the three of us, we ended up with quite the concoction of hatred and bitterness. Everyone in my family tells me Daddy is just supporting me to get back at Mom for their divorce. But I don't believe that's true. Even if it were, at least he was my ticket out of the marriage.

I keep my phone under the table as I message my dad

back. After all, since this is the last mediation of our divorce, I am supposed to be listening to what is going to be my future.

"I guess I'm ok, Dad. It's not going exactly how I wanted."

"What do you mean, sweetie?" he replies.

"We've agreed to joint custody with 50/50 time and child support. We're going to sell our house and I can continue to live in Florence, but since we are sharing 50/50 time, living further than the hour-long drive I currently have is out of the question . . . at least for now."

"What are you going to do about the girls' school situation?"

"The girls will continue going to the ministry's elementary school. On my days I will have to commute with them to school, then head to work in the mornings." It's several minutes before I hear a reply.

"You have to get those girls out of there, Lindsey. Your mother calls herself a 'minister' but she's a tyrant, and that place she's created for herself is a cult. You and the girls can't continue to stay around people who will ultimately brainwash you and them. Casey can't raise two girls and he knows that. This is about power and him being able to save face and keep his position. I'm sure your mom is in there on the phone with him right now. They've planned this whole thing out against you, even from the beginning."

"I don't know what to do, Dad. If I keep fighting for custody this will go to a courtroom. We have to settle today." I am hoping I can be left alone to return to my thoughts. He replies one last time. "Then you try to take him for all he's worth. Over time he will tire of the responsibility of raising two girls and he'll end up abusing and abandoning them like he did you. When that happens you'll get them for good and you can get them away from that monster and that place. Joyce and I are praying for you right now. God will make you to come out on top."

Come out on top . . . I see no top here to be had. Is there any win in a divorce? None that I can see. Our girls, our two beautiful girls—they will be crushed when this is over. My bronze-haired, blue-eyed Analeise who is two months shy of turning nine is going to have her first birthday without a solid, secure family. She's been praying and believing, journaling and begging me to call off the divorce. Then there's my sweet little Katie bug, Casey's carbon copy. At five-years-old she will not remember me and Casey together. She won't remember us being a family. They're so young—too young—and I can tell the last two years are starting to take their toll on them.

The day continues to go by in a daze. I eventually find myself in another room of the courthouse facing Casey and his attorney. Before our mediation can be over we have to record the settlement as well as put it on paper. Great, something else to make this day even longer.

The mediator's voice begins. "Mr. Doss, for record purposes please state your name."

"Casey Allen Doss," Casey replies. His voice is different. Hurt . . . but something else too. I almost want to say relieved.

"Mrs. Doss, your full name please."

"Lindsey Reneé Doss." Doss. The sound of my last name sticks in my head. I will have to officially change my last name back to Wheaton. I've been unofficially going by my maiden name for a while now. Or simply Lindsey Reneé. But today makes it a bit more real. Not much longer now and we will sign. Then it will be only a short time before the judge gets to our papers and he signs as well. After that, it's over.

The mediator begins going over the seemingly endless settlement details. ". . . Casey will have the girls three-and-a-half days, and Lindsey will have them three-and-a-half days. Christmas will be alternated every other year with Lindsey taking even years and Casey taking odd. Lindsey has both children on her birthday, Mother's Day and half of the girls' birthdays, Casey will have both children on his birthday, Father's Day and half of the girls' birthdays . . ." On and on and on it goes; everything from the custody arrangement to assets to financial settlements.

Casey is in his usual position, leaned back in his chair, arms crossed, chewing the inside of his cheek as he always does when he is in deep thought. He must feel me staring because he looks over at me . . . his eyes. For a moment my heart skips a beat. I glance away quickly and try to stop the pounding that is happening in my chest. Oh, those piercing, dark blue eyes. Usually so full of love, but today they're agonizingly painful, empty except for unutterable hurt. So sad. So hopeless. Like he's just taken a bullet and I'm the one who has pulled the trigger. Was this me? Did I do this? Was it me who wounded him? Why am I doing this? It's been so long I don't remember now.

After everything is said and done—after the emotions of our separation and divorce proceedings run their course—it's hard to remember what got us here in the first place. Has it really been almost two years since we separated and I filed for this divorce? It seems like it was just yesterday.

I should be listening to the settlement to make sure his lawyer doesn't try to put something into the recording without my consent. But I can't. I'm too tired now to care. I just want to go home. Be alone. Precisely what I wanted, right? To be alone?

Part of me wants to stand up here and now and call the whole thing off. Maybe give us a little more time to see what can happen. The other part of me is so tired of it all that I'm just ready for it to be over. Even if it's the wrong decision, I want it to be done. The stress has been unbearable. Having to answer everyone's questions has almost driven me mad, especially when the answers have to keep changing to support the lies I created.

What am I saying? How did I let myself get this far gone? How did I turn into this? How have I been thinking and believing so terribly of him? I mean, I still want the marriage to be over, I guess . . . but then again, I don't. This isn't what I wanted. This loneliness and numbness is not what I expected it to be. It is not the picture I had in my mind of "being free." The separation and beginning days of the divorce were everything I thought they would be. But now, life is very different. I wanted to hurt him, to drive the sword in as deep as I could. Heaven knows I've succeeded there. How did I allow myself to become so bitter, so angry? It was like the "Mr. Hyde" side of me has completely taken over. To be honest, I don't know who I am anymore. Or what I want. Maybe I never did. Maybe this was all done on a whim. Maybe it will be the worst decision I've ever made. Maybe it really will turn out all right in the end, and I'll get what I originally thought I wanted: freedom and happiness. Or maybe I won't get either one of those.

Knowing we will still be here for a while longer, I continue to let my thoughts of self-pity wander until they land on the one day that started me on this dreadful path. The day I turned into a monster.

Chapter 3

DECISIONS

March 17th, 2014. Casey calls me into the great room of our home. Technically it's not ours. We own a smaller house that we rent out on the other side of our small town. The house we currently live in is just a rental from a family friend. We needed somewhere bigger for the time being. It is the largest and nicest house we've had so far. Hand-painted murals on the walls, a playroom for the girls, a stunning master suite, and an even more stunning great room. We've lived here a little over a year and had planned on purchasing it soon.

I'm already exhausted from the conversation we've not even had. Casey says he wants to have these talks to try and "heal our marriage", but I know that's a lie. He is just wearing me down, trying to pin me into a corner and show off his great "I know more than you, I'm right and you're wrong" power. This isn't about love. This is about his position with the ministry and, more than that, it's about him needing to put his thumb on top of someone.

Well, it's not going to be me. Not anymore. It took me two years and the help of the people who really care about me to see the truth and realize I was living in a bad situation. Things have been pretty bad for a while now. I moved many of my clothes to the guest room of our house and have been sleeping there for close to a year.

After her singing career, my mother launched The Ramp, a large youth ministry in Hamilton, Alabama, also known as "No-wheres-ville USA." I am director of everything that involves dance and theater there, including all choreography and management for the traveling ministry team, *Chosen.* Casey is the pastor of Ramp Church and the Ramp School of Ministry director. Needless to say the family/ministry/work dynamic complicates things quite a bit. I am forbidden by the ministry to speak of our problems to anyone. Not because of anything they are trying to hide; just what they are trying to protect. And that would be Casey. I'm trapped. Miserable. For anyone to know we are having marital problems jeopardizes the reputation of the ministry and calls Casey's own reputation and name into question. I have no one I can trust. Everyone is connected to this place or to my mother in some way. I feel like every ministry we are close to betrays me. We've been to six counselors, all of them being people my mother knows or can get a hold of; all of them somehow ending up telling her just enough to know what I've shared with them. She in turn confronts me and tells me repeatedly how my life will be utterly ruined and I will lose everything with this choice. To her, this is in no way the will of God for my life. Who is she to say what the will of God is for me? She is not God! And I can hear from Him on my own just fine, thank you very much.

No one is safe. Not even my mother. In the past I have tried talking to a few other ministers or counselors we know about the disagreements Casey and I have had, trying desperately to have just one of them hear out my side of things and understand that the arguments Casey and I have really are controlling and abusive; that the situation I am in really is dire. But not a single person sees it that way. Apparently they don't believe it is controlling to speak your mind and demand that your wife stop secretly talking to her dance partner until the wee hours of the morning, or that she be home to make dinner and not be out with her young, single friends. I write that off to all of them trying to protect Mom and the ministry. But not me. No one protects me. I am on my own.

I walk into the great room where Casey has just called me, and stand in front of him with my arms crossed. I'm hoping he will not see the fear beginning to take me over—fear that I might really lose the things in my life that are most important to me; my perfect Neverland world I've worked so hard to create, my job, my dreams . . . I'm afraid I will lose my best friend and dance partner, Tristan. I call him Tree. To him, I am Bird—a fitting name for someone in need of wings.

I can feel the ultimatum coming and I know Casey is

going to make me choose between my marriage and what I really want: my freedom, my happiness. Freedom from him, freedom from the ministry, freedom from this whole wretched place, and everyone in it. The price of freedom is so high, though. Am I really willing to pay it? I will lose my reputation, my credibility; any honor I have left will be gone. I will be seen as "the woman with the scarlet letter." I can't let that happen, but how do I get free without all the collateral damage that will follow?

To stay with Casey means I will never be free. He will never let me work with Tristan again. He will never let me have the dance career I have trained and worked for the past ten years to have. He will demand I "grow up" and "become responsible" and make him, my home, my kids the SOLE PRIORITY of my life. How does he not see I am so much more than just a housewife and mom? Besides, have I not already done "wife" things? The house stays clean, as best as I can keep it at least. The job I have had at the ministry pays well; I've already separated my money from his and begun paying for my own car and phone. He is there after school to take care of the girls while I am running rehearsals and choreography. Does he just not want to be with his kids?

I've spent nine years being his "Stepford Wife", making all his meals, washing his clothes, and taking care of his home. I don't have people here visiting when he's home. I wear headphones while I work writing dances all evening so the noise won't bother him. And yeah, Tristan and I talk and spend almost all day every day together, but we don't always work alone. Besides, what we do is work related and we've not done anything physical. Not even romantic! And even if there were feelings there they would never be spoken out loud. He's my best friend, for crying out loud! Does Casey really expect me to give up my best friend? Nothing has ever happened between Tristan and me, despite the concerns many people have had about the closeness of our friendship. What else could I do for Casey to be what he calls "a good wife"?

I *know* God Himself has called me to the dance world and to eventually create a dance company and school for all people—*that* is my true calling, not waiting on Casey hand and foot. It's what Tristan and I have been talking about doing together for years: starting an amazing dance school and company. If Casey doesn't want to be a part of what God called his own wife to do then it's his problem, not mine. But he will miss out. And he will hold me back.

Casey wants out of the marriage. In my heart I know he does. He just won't say it himself. After all, if people saw that he was really the one who wanted out of the marriage he would lose everything, and heaven forbid people see his true colors. Why won't he just go ahead and file for a divorce himself? I've been starving him of affection for months now hoping to speed up the process, sometimes going weeks at a time without speaking even a single word to him, despite us living under the same roof with two young girls. It is pure stubbornness keeping him here now. He tries to be sweet to me but it's only so he can tell people all the wonderful and kind things he is doing while I am, as he says, "so cold" back to him. He doesn't mean a single bit of his "kindness."

How can a husband look at his wife that he "loves" and tell her to "not act in ways that are beneath her", and then turn around and try to be kind to her? That's how I know it's fake. How can one make the demands he makes on my time and when I'm home? How can a man tell his wife who her best friend can or cannot be? Is that not control? From what I have researched it is. I have every right to leave an unhappy and toxic marriage. Ultimately God wants me to be happy. People would understand that. They would have to. Sure, some will not believe me, but those are the ones who are blinded by his flawless platform personality and by the influence of my mother and her ministry.

After several moments of awkward silence and the stonewalling routine I finally have down pat, Casey starts in on me. "Lindsey, I love you and I want to make this work, but I can't live in a marriage sharing my wife with another man. I can't live in a marriage where we live two separate lives. I want us to be one, to be best friends. I want us to work together and enjoy life together. I am willing, and want, to do whatever we have to do to heal our marriage. But for this to work, you will have to cut Tristan completely off. I don't want just half of you, and I'm not going to share your time or attention with him."

I stand there silently for several moments, eyes down, desperately trying to get away from his gaze.

He has been questioning me about Tristan for a long time. For years it has bothered him that we are so close. It bothers him that we sometimes practice alone despite his requests for us not to. But what am I supposed to do? Cancel our rehearsal time together? It bothers him that our partnering requires Tristan to put his hands on my waist or leg or wherever he has to in order to perform a lift, but none of it is done in a romantic manner. It is just to get our job done. And Casey certainly would never partner with me. So, obviously, partnering with someone else is the only option I have. As for the closeness of our friendship, it is impossible to spend that much time with someone and not be close. I don't understand why he wouldn't want us close if we have to work together like we do. If I were completely honest, I would much rather be hanging out with Tristan over Casey any day. He keeps it fun and magical and free from responsibility.

Deep down, I feel the shaking starting to come. I know where this is going, so I coldly glare at him. "You're not going to control me and tell me who my friends can or can't be," I snap back.

"He is not 'just your friend,' Lindsey. He's not been 'just your friend' for a long time. And no, this is not control. This is reasonable for any marriage. You're not going to be with me and have this fantasy world you live in with some other man on the side who you say is 'just your dance partner and friend.' We met with him, Lindsey. We know things have crossed over the line." Hearing of them meeting with Tristan and remembering what they did to him rouses my anger. They fired him, exiled him, broke his heart. They forbade him to ever speak or respond to me or contact me in any way again. I will never forgive them for it.

I swiftly give my answer before I become too afraid to say anything at all or, even worse, stay with him out of fear and pity. "Then my answer is no. I'm not going to give in to your abusive and controlling demands, and I'm not giving up my *friend.*" There. I said it. Casey turns his head and bites down on his jaw. He is angry . . . no, he is hurt . . . he's devastated beyond words. Well . . . good. I feel all the conflicting voices creeping back up: telling me to stay, telling me to go. I feel the prick of the Spirit convicting me, but I am going to hold my ground. After all, it's not like he's really going to do anything that drastic about it, and it's not like it's really *all* my fault, right?

Next comes the final blow I don't expect. "Then you have to make your choice, Lindsey. I want you, more than anything. I want our marriage. I want this to work. I want you to stay. But I can't keep living like we have. You can stay, but you will have to cut off Tristan. We can put our lives back together, we will heal our marriage. Or, you can go. But it is going to be your choice. And if you choose to go, understand that this is never, *never* what I wanted. I would be . . ."

"Fine, I'll leave," I interrupt. "*You* are the one that doesn't want this. *You* are the one that doesn't want me. So since you are kicking me out without any legitimate cause at all, I'll go." I turn and walk out of the room, leaving him to think about what he has done to me.

I can't believe it. This is actually happening. We are separating. I have been waiting on this moment for months now. I've been talking about it to Dad, both of us just waiting for when I can be free. Now, all of a sudden that moment is here. I wish I were relieved . . . but surprisingly I'm not. I am scared to death. What will I do? So many questions flood my mind all at once. I have never been on my own before. I married Casey right out of high school. I don't know how to take care of myself! I've only worked for my mother and her ministry. I've never had to worry about bills or deadlines or late fees. I've never had to call insurance companies or buy a house! Casey always took care of those things. I've never had to be alone. In theory, alone sounds great! But now, I start to question my decisions.

I am expecting him to come into our bedroom with me, maybe to talk again, to apologize for what he just did. I really don't want him to because I don't want to hear anything he has to say. But, then again, I am desperate to see him standing in the door. Nothing happens. He really means it. The time has come and I have to make my choice.

"Stay, Lindsey. You don't want to do this," comes the

still small voice within me. For a moment I consider it. For a moment I stop and turn around, contemplating his offer. Forget it. What can I say or do, anyway? He's been done for a long, long time. I know he has. I have to believe that, despite what he says or does, and now he has just kicked me out of our house, and for no reason. I've done nothing wrong to him! At least, not by what most people define as 'wrong'.

The girls . . . what are they going to say? What will they think? They are going to be crushed. They will be devastated when they come home from school and Mommy and Daddy are not together anymore. The stress they've been living in has been bad enough but this puts a whole new spin on things for them. What will he tell them? I will have to handle it first—before he destroys them, too.

I throw some clothes into a large suitcase, walk out and slam the door behind me. I am completely unaware of the man I've spent the last decade of my life with weeping in our living room, begging God to make the pain stop and to heal our family.

I will need to get the girls from school before he does. I will have just enough time to tell my mother how Casey made ridiculous controlling demands, and said I could only be friends with who *he* wanted, told me I had to quit my job at her ministry so that I could serve and wait on him, was horribly cruel and verbally abusive, and said all but how much he hates me. Then when I said "no" to his demands, he kicked me out.

Jumping into my small, white car I head to my mother's house. As much as I want to message Tristan, I can't. There are too many people who would pry around and ask him if we've talked. Casey will probably start stalking my phone records as well; he never has before but who knows. So calling Tristan will be out of the question. I decide instead to send him a quick Snapchat of me in my car with my bags, hoping he will take the hint without me having to say anything. At least that way he can say we never actually talked. He checked it. Good. He may not know exactly what is happening but he may have some form of a clue. As soon as I see the 'x' beside his name, I know he has screenshot the pic. It's his way of responding back. I delete my Snapchat feed so no one can look up my recent history, then delete the app. It gets exhausting having to delete and re-load these apps in order to communicate with him in secret but it's worth it. And it won't last forever.

I text my father, my lifeline: "It's begun, Dad. Casey kicked me out. He actually kicked me out. You're right. He is a monster. You wouldn't believe how he talked to me. Like I was a piece of trash. His control is beyond anything I've ever seen. How can he do this to me?" My father replies, "Oh Sweetie, my sweet baby girl. It is going to be ok. You are going to get through this. But honey, it is going to get worse before it gets better." Another message comes in before I can reply. "Be prepared, Lindsey. Your mother will turn against you too."

Oh please. She is my mother, for crying out loud. I know we don't agree on where the marriage has been lately but she would NEVER abandon me. She may be mad and disappointed but she will have to take my side, especially when I tell her what Casey has done today. Pulling into her driveway, I don't have time to answer Daddy back. Eyes red from my tears of self-pity (and a hint of self-loathing I force myself to shove down), I take my suitcase and knock on her door.

"Hey, Lindsey," she says coldly. Odd. Maybe she had a bad day—as if anyone's day could be worse than mine. "Casey called. We need to talk."

No. Surely not! He didn't actually stoop so low as to get to my own mother first? There's no way. I can't believe this. All of a sudden it's as if I can see into the future, the whole thing playing out. My father was right—this is a set up. They are going to play me as the fool, the harlot, the sinner, the one who left her perfect little catalogue family. Something snaps within me. Oh, I am done all right. I am done with all of them. They have no idea what I have become. And unfortunately, neither do I.

Chapter 4

HOW IT ALL STARTED

My path started not with my own divorce but with the one that occurred between my parents when I was only eight. A child learns behaviors and develops core values and mindsets from watching their parents. If a healthy home is not shown, even if just by one parent, that child will grow up believing that way of life is normal. Children of a divorced home will most assuredly begin to act out as a result of the stresses of their environment.

Unless you've been there, it's hard to understand what it does to a child's mind when their parents split up. All your security is gone. You feel unprotected. Betrayed. Confused. Devastated beyond words. You don't have the emotional capacity to handle seeing one (or both) of your parents hurting so bad or being hostile toward each other. Then, in thinking you will try to help them be happy, you unintentionally put on a smile and push your own feelings aside blocking out the pain; shoving all the hurt into a bottle inside you and corking it tight. All of those un-dealt-with emotions may hide well for a time but, eventually, at the first sign of a conflict or confrontation, they will most certainly come pouring out.

As a child in a divorce situation, you don't understand the "who is right" and "who is wrong." Even if one parent did terrible things to the other, that is not the parent you know. Your relationship with them is totally different. So to hear of them in a negative manner or to hear the things they did to the other parent hurts deeply and is very, very confusing.

Sadly, so many people have come from a broken home as a child, that going through another divorce in their own lives is not even that big of a deal. It's just a divorce, right? The kids will adjust and move forward just like the parents will. After all, we turned out ok after our own parents' divorce, didn't we? However, we have all become so good at turning our pain into baggage that not many realize the psychological and emotional damage it inflicts on the lives of kids and parents, and, in most cases, coming from a divorced home drastically increases the chances of you going through a divorce yourself. Then that divorce raises the chances for your kids, and their kids— and so the cycle goes on. Then you find your family locked in a generational curse of broken hearts and broken families, just from the next generation growing up thinking a divorce is a normal part of life.

When everything hits the fan and the marriage ends it is NEVER blamed on the trauma of the previous divorce we went through as kids when our own families were torn apart. It is blamed on something the other person did. Because, after all, we could never have done anything so wrong that it ended the marriage. But if everything is perfect, why is there a divorce? If I grew up and moved on and "healed" from my parents' divorce, why are my spouse and I arguing over all the baggage I brought into the marriage? If I have baggage, where did it come from? Could it be that the divorces some of us walked through as kids and teenagers set us on a path of pain and trauma, thus resulting in poor choices and consequences that cost us our own happiness and peace? In reality, a divorce could be the leading cause of every other divorce that happens.

As of today, the primary reason for divorce in America is communication issues, followed by adultery, then financial disagreements. But how did the communication issues begin? If you really think about it, it is easy to believe we have them from infancy. Children are a blank slate on which parents write every day. They grow up and adopt the behaviors and habits they see in the home. If there is strife in the home they view that as normal. If the mother and father don't get along, and have friendships or relationships outside of the marriage, most likely the child will grow up and think that is normal; or, on the flip side, they will be so angry they will find themselves spiraling downward so hard and fast that they themselves will end up in a slew of relationships, committing to anyone who comes along just because they saw it so abused and destroyed in their own parents' lives. But that lifestyle ends with baggage from sleeping around and its own trail of shame; baggage and shame that is, in turn, taken into another marriage. That marriage ends, leaving more baggage and shame and trauma for the children involved there. What are we teaching our children about covenant and love? About security and protection? About marriage and family?

Don't get me wrong, I know many children who grew up with divorced parents and turned out healed and whole, with no problems at all. But, by and large, the majority of kids grow up facing many issues that surrounded that first divorce. I also know there are situations in which a divorce is inevitable and sometimes necessary for the protection of the children and spouse. However, too often we throw away a marriage because of things like communication, financial disagreements, and accusations of abuse that is really not abuse at all. When there is legitimate danger or adultery or abandonment involved, the decision is then left to the couple, and the Lord will back that decision. Things like communication issues or society's incredibly broad definition of "verbal and emotional abuse" are neither life-threatening nor necessary for a divorce. Are they hard? Without question. Are they wrong? Yes, but it is no reason to cut the marriage off. The excuses of "we can't talk or agree on anything" or

"I'm unhappy and the kids don't need to grow up in an unhappy home," or the most common one, "He is manipulating and controlling me and what he says to me is abusive" is *NO* excuse. Many times these justifications are not based in reality, they are simply a way to defend our bad choices or cover up the real reasons we want out of the marriage.

We need whole and redeemed homes, not excuses for our wrong behaviors. Redemption may not be easy, and redemption may not always work, but it is always the right thing to try—and REALLY try. Don't give it 10 percent, but try with everything in you. Because, at the end of the day, you and your children will be living with the consequences of whatever choice you make for your family; and, whatever the outcome, you have to be able to say you fought with everything within you.

This fight is not over a contract—it is over a covenant. A contract means "I will take a bullet for you," but a covenant says, "I will take a bullet *from* you."

What would happen in families if the divorce statistic changed to say 10, or even 20, percent with the leading cause being an actual court-documented, proven domestic violence case, (not "oh, he abused me" because he said something you didn't like), or real, legitimate infidelity or abandonment? What if divorce were not even allowed unless the two parties were only given "adultery" or "domestic violence" as the grounds to end it? Not "irreconcilable differences" or the "no fault" divorce.

What if people were first required to separate for at least a year before being allowed to file? What if they were required to get real help from counselors and had to try and fix their marriage before a divorce was granted? Would the crime rate drop? Would the prison population drop? Would domestic violence itself go down? Because, after all, if a child grows up in a healthy and whole home, chances are that same child would strive to have a healthy, whole home too. Would the adultery rate drop? When, in a couple of generations from now, children grow up in whole homes, with parents who fought to make it work and put each other first, would all of those statistics go down? One thing is for certain: after a couple of generations of a virtually divorce-free society, "communication issues" would not even be on the radar. Couples would be forced to face each other, talk about and fix their issues. There'd be no way out at that point, especially if it couldn't be used as a reason for divorce. Couples would have to stick it out and make it work. Would it be easy? No. It would be hard, and it would take hard work. It would mean listening to and learning from each other, and fighting through a lot of baggage. But would it not be worth it?

The thought of such a life is a beautiful thing, but to walk out that commitment is very different. It takes much responsibility: having to face yourself and fix your own problems before pointing a finger at the other. It means growing up, being an adult, and owning up to our choices. For the most part, running away is so much easier so that is the path we choose. Instead of facing and fixing our problems we choose to run, we choose to escape. This escape, the fantasy and lie we create for ourselves, opens up the door for the most destructive weapon in the enemy's arsenal.

Chapter 5

FREEDOM

My eyes open earlier than normal. I desperately want to close them again and disappear from this day or, even better, life altogether. Fear, anger, hatred, relief . . . maybe self-loathing; I don't really know what emotion is coursing through me. It's all kind of a toss-up on the day you're scheduled to file for a divorce.

Almost a month has gone by. Casey doesn't know I have been back and forth to Florence a few times now to meet with my attorney. Dad says I should go ahead and be the one to get the divorce going. We all know it's going to happen anyway so why wait. Part of me thinks I should wait and continue to try and provoke Casey to file, but who knows if he ever would, and really I just want to be free. It is time to get it all over with and get on with my life. My problem now is that if I cannot give a good enough reason to leave the marriage, or prove him to be an unfit parent (which unfortunately he is not), we will end up with split custody. If that happens I will never get to leave this area. I will be stuck here for another ten years or more. Maybe, just maybe, I can prove him to be unfit in some way beyond actual parenting. Dad has reassured me there are many things for which we could pin him to the wall like a bug. If I can do that, even if I don't get sole physical and legal custody, at least I could possibly get enough to escape. My father had the brief idea to arrange a second marriage as soon as our papers are signed. He says it would give the court a reason to let me move the girls out of state and I could have it annulled immediately after. Needless to say, that is not going to happen. We can find a better way.

Many of my close friends have listened to my stories of Casey and our arguments over Tristan and my "obsession" with my job. They all agree that Casey's demands are controlling. They're also all people who already don't like him and who hate my mother and the ministry. I had to have a support group and, since my own family turned on me, this group of people that already hate them were the only option I had. They were the only ones who wouldn't betray my words, actions or whereabouts to my family.

What kind of person tries to steal their spouse's family? I already know the answer: the one that, if exposed, would have far too much to lose. They will see the truth, though. Casey will reveal himself at some point during this whole process and they will finally see what I see: a tyrant.

Why should I even care what they see, though? Why does it matter what they believe? Who even cares if they side with him or not? If they do side with him maybe they'll come crashing down too, and then I would have a double win under my belt. But why do I want my mother's approval and pat on the back so bad? Why do I need her support? I am an adult! I can do whatever I want! As much as I don't want to admit it, I desperately need her to believe me. I am terrified of her, of what she will say about me. She can do so much damage and people will take her word over mine any day. She holds my entire identity, and if I lose that then I'm done.

I sit in my house putting on my shoes to go tell Casey my plans for the outcome of the marriage, to tell him that I am in fact ending the marriage today. As I open my door I look back over my shoulder and gaze up at my house. It's the first house Casey and I bought together. We didn't want to sell it completely after we moved into our current home so we kept it and have been renting it out ever since. Good thing too, otherwise I would have had nowhere to go. It's like God knew I would need a place to stay eventually and made sure we still had this house available. This is a cute little home, tucked away nicely on a hill in the woods. It's small, but very quaint. We were so happy when we bought it . . .

I remember we were driving around town looking at various spots of land and homes, as we always did on Sunday afternoons. A "For Sale" sign caught our attention. We drove down the long, winding driveway until we came to the top of a hill. "Surely it's not that house, it's beautiful!"

I said to Casey. We parked in the driveway and walked around the property. It was early spring and buttercups were forming a large yellow blanket in the big front yard. The old brick was covered with lush green ivy on one side and sported tall white columns on the front porch. We definitely didn't want this house to get away from us so we quickly called to see if it was in our budget. There are few really nice homes in Hamilton so one must grab them quickly when they become available. I couldn't believe it when we were actually signing the deed to OUR house a couple of weeks later. It was our very first house. Prior to this we had rented a small home close to my mother, but with the two girls it was quickly outgrown. This house was perfect for us—perfect size, perfect location. We were happy at this house.

Now it's empty. Bare walls. Nothing left but memories. I wonder where Casey will end up going when this is over? He won't be able to stay at our current home alone. My guess is he will take one of Mom's many fully-furnished ministry properties. Good for him. He gets a new house— mortgage free, probably—*and* my family. My attorney's recommendation is to go ahead and take residence in this house after we separated, since the previous tenants have been gone for a while now. I moved back in here when life at Mom's house became too stressful, which took only a few days. My name is on the deed after all, so he can't technically kick me out of this home, and he can't sell or rent it without my consent. For now I will have a secure place to stay until then. At least it leaves me with our furniture and several more of our assets.

Closing my car door, I head out to have the one meeting I know will change everything. Today will change my status at the ministry, my relationship with Mom, how everyone views me, and who I am—everything. After today there is no turning back. Once the divorce is filed and in the system it is a process to get it stopped, or so I've been told. He can't just ignore it, and if he does for more than thirty days, I am granted everything I am asking for. Maybe that will happen. Maybe he will wait for a "miracle" and wait too long. And nothing will have to go to court and I can simply take the girls and walk away. But that's unlikely. The ministers and leaders counseling Casey right now would never let that happen.

My appointment is soon and it is an hour's drive to my attorney's office. I will have to be quick at Casey's house. Part of me wants to skip this conversation with him, go straight to her office and have the papers presented to Casey without me having to tell him myself. I don't want to face him again, but I know the right thing to do is to go to his house in person and at least let him know the marriage is ending. He doesn't need to be hanging on to false hope that we can stay together so he can continue to live his "perfect family" façade. He only wants the marriage to look good for his audience anyway. It has nothing to do with loving me.

When I knock on the door of our large home, a simple

"Come in" is all I hear. Casey is sitting on our living room couch, the very first piece of furniture we bought as a newly-wed couple. It used to hold us as we cuddled together. It is where I sat and nursed my two girls. It is where he would sit with his feet propped up, drinking Pepsi, and watching basketball. Now it will be the place I end our marriage. I walk over and sit silently on the cushion furthest from him. Several silent moments pass before he speaks.

"Just answer me this one question, Lindsey: why? Why are you doing this to us?" Casey asks, tears beginning to stream down his pale face. "I don't understand why you don't even want to try. Do you not want the marriage at all?"

His tears are killing me. It hurts seeing him in so much pain. Knowing it is about to get a lot worse I will have to keep a straight face. I have to stay strong through this.

"No, Casey. I don't want the marriage, and you don't want it either," I reply. It feels like a dagger going through me as soon as I hear the words leave my mouth.

"That is not true, Lindsey. You know that is not true. What will I tell the girls? How can you let this happen to them?"

"Tell them whatever you want, Casey. Tell them whatever story you want to tell them and I'll tell them my own. The girls will be fine. Divorces happen every day and kids survive them. They will grow up and move on from this. They will get over it soon enough." Another dagger. I know I will not be able to be here much longer or I will be reduced to tears myself. And I can't show any weakness.

A dark voice takes over my thoughts: *"This is what he really wants, Lindsey. He just won't admit to it. He's lying when he says he wants to make the marriage work. You know he is. All he wants is to look right for everyone in the ministry. That's why he won't admit to wanting the divorce. You have to do the dirty work so he can walk away clean, but truth will win out one day. Wait and see. He'll expose himself eventually."*

But could it work? He looks like he really actually loves me. Maybe I was wrong. Maybe he does care more than I thought.

"That's exactly what he wants you to think. He is a marvelous actor, but that's not real love. If he really loved you he wouldn't try to control and manipulate you like he did."

I can't stay. I can't live in a cage forever. I can't live the life I really want and am supposed to have with the ties he is putting on me. If I stay I will never be free. I am stronger than this. Those tears are fake. He's putting on his show. It won't work on me.

"End it."

Just a couple of more minutes, maybe I don't have to do this.

"End it now."

I can't do it.

"Lose him or lose your hard-fought freedom."

Stoically I hear the sentence leave my lips. "I am leaving today to file for a divorce." Did I just hear myself say that

I was filing for a divorce? This can't be real. But it is. I can't inhale. I can't exhale. I can't do anything but sit there, staring at him.

The statement hits him like a sack of bricks. "So you're not even going to try? You won't give us our best chance? You're going to end everything? You don't know what you're doing, Lindsey. Don't do this."

"I have to do this. I have to, for me and for the girls. You don't want to try." I answer back. "I know you don't." I am suffocating in this room. I stand and start to walk out before I stop breathing completely, or worse, cry.

"Lindsey . . ." he calls to me. Head high, face set, I turn around. "I love you, Lindsey. Everyone and everything aside, I will still fight for you and for us. I love you so much." I hear myself slam the door behind me, and my footsteps echoing off the pavement. My body is shaking so badly I can hardly stand. My heart is pounding in my ears and I can feel a cold chill creeping down my spine.

"Lindsey, stop."

I ignore that still, small voice I've known so well. This voice, however, has grown fainter and fainter over the past month.

"Go back, Lindsey."

Finally the tension erupts out of me. "NO, God! NO! I won't go back! For once in my life I am going to do what *I* want! And NO ONE is going to tell me otherwise! You want me to be happy, don't you, God? Well, that's exactly what I am going to do. I am going to be happy. I am going to have *my* friends, *my* career, *MY LIFE*, no matter what!"

"*This will cost you everything. It will leave you empty, Lindsey.*"

Then so be it. I enter my car and turn my music up to drown out the conviction trying to take over me. I drive the hour and fifteen minutes to Florence to file the papers that will change my life forever.

Chapter 6

FILING

"So you are ready to get this going?" my attorney, Dianne, asks a couple of hours later.

"Yes," I reply. I wait in the cold leather chair as she gathers the paperwork.

"You can still walk out."

I don't want to walk out.

"Don't do this."

I have to do this. Someone else will love me, really love me.

"He already loves you."

"Stop questioning yourself, Lindsey," I keep telling myself. "You have to go through with it. You're too far in to turn back now. You've come too far. What will your father think if you turn back now? He fronted all the attorney's fees, supported you, cried with you, prayed for you, opened up his home . . . what about all the people who have stood with you? If you turn back now you'll lose them all and they're the only real friends you have. Do you not remember how bad it has been for the past several years? Casey tried to control you; he was the one holding you back from everything you're supposed to be. He's the one pitting your own mother and sister against you!"

I think back to the night we separated, when Casey presented his ultimatum and then kicked me out of the house, and I let the anger and hatred fill me again. I think about driving to Mom's and realizing he got to her first. I think about those few days at her house and having to sit through the endless talks she had with me about how I am "out of the will of God and will lose everything" if I do this. I think about sitting through her analogies of how there is a storm in the spirit realm and how it is going to come and hit my house. Ridiculous. I feel the hatred I have for them rising and remember this really is worth it. This is happening because of them. They teamed up with their stories and lies and turned me into the monster. Then they turned around and tried to kill what they created. In reality, this is entirely their fault, not mine. They made me this way. They turned me into this dark, embittered creature, and now they will go to any length to get rid of me. Create me, then kill me—it's what they do to anyone who doesn't fit their mold or believe and behave in a manner they find acceptable.

Even though I am starting to see the truth of everyone's motives, I'm not sure why I still can't get the conflicting voices out of my head. One pleading, "Go back to him, Lindsey. You can make this right. It's worth it," and the other interrupting with, "Run, Lindsey. Run as hard as you can away from him and that place. Be free for once in your life." Now those voices are almost more than I can stand.

My attorney strides over to where I am sitting in her small office. "This is the petition for divorce we will be sending," she says. "According to our previous consultations we are petitioning for you to have sole physical and legal custody, monthly child and spousal support, half of all marital assets, and the rights for you to leave Alabama and live within a day's drive. This will hopefully allow you to go ahead and move to Florida with your father. Look it over one last time before you sign." I glance quickly over the papers. To be honest, I really don't care what they say as long as I can get free of Casey, Mom and that horrible place. From what I do read, Dianne has included all my accusations against Casey; the only reasons I can conjure up to get the divorce without looking like the bad guy. Abuse: verbal, mental, and physical. Deep down, as much as I don't want to admit it, I know they're all lies. But I have to have a way out. I will have to lie. I know there has never been any abuse, but there is nothing else I can use. It is my easiest way out. Who cares that it might destroy his name? He'll bounce back.

I have nothing that would constitute a biblical divorce. People would never believe me if I accused him of something like adultery. He has stayed completely faithful to me in thought and action. But abuse—maybe, just maybe that will be believable enough to cover my tracks. Maybe it will be enough to keep people from pointing their finger at me.

If anyone really knew that freedom and happiness, a dance career and, more than anything, being able to keep Tristan in my life is my real motive behind wanting out of my marriage, my life would never be the same. My attorney is very optimistic that we can word the papers in a way that will create enough doubt that he 'seems' abusive. After all, he did hold my arm once when we were arguing. Really, it was more like my hand . . . but what's the difference? He was mad because I had been away from the home, him, and the girls for months while directing my department's fall dinner theater and spending countless hours with Tristan. Deep down I knew I needed to go home more. I knew there were rehearsals and meetings I didn't have to be at. I knew I should have been with the girls. But he should have understood my commitment to my job and picked up the slack. When he asked me to come home and be with him and the girls instead of spending the evening at an after party with my friends I got angry and turned to walk away from him. He held on to my hand to try to finish talking to me. I immediately jerked my arm away in a fit, causing as much of a scene as possible, and went straight to my friends to tell them what he did. Totally abusive—even they agreed it was. After all, any physical contact when someone is upset is an act of aggression, right?

Along with that accusation Dianne included Casey closing the door behind us in the bedroom (actually so the girls wouldn't walk in) while he tried pleading with me about the marriage. He was in front of the door and I couldn't walk out. He was desperately trying to keep me in the conversation since I always refused to talk about anything pertaining to him and me. That incident could be considered restraining and locking someone in a room if worded the right way. Lucky for me, my attorney has done just that.

"The papers look good to me," I say.

"Wonderful!" she replies. "Last but not least, how would you like for these to be sent? They can be mailed to his PO Box or be served to him by the sheriff."

I think for a moment. "Which is faster?" I ask her.

She smiles. "Well, they're both about the same, but if I were you, I would have the sheriff deliver them. It is far more humiliating, especially if everyone in the city knows who he and your mother are. It's more of a slap in the face."

I smirk back at her. "Let's do that then." What have I turned into? I'm not this heartless. This isn't me. Or is it? I hear that still, small voice and Romans 1:24 rings through my mind. *"So God abandoned them to do whatever shameful things their hearts desired . . ."*

That does not refer to me, God. I know that's not me. I've not turned on You! Just my husband! This can be forgiven. I can ask for forgiveness for all the lying and for the divorce later. It is not the unpardonable sin. I'm still trying to find out if it's even a sin at all!

My attorney finishes gathering the paperwork. "I need you to sign here, please, Lindsey," she says casually. She hands me a pen. I look down at the line bearing my printed name and the title "Petitioner." I know the minute my name is written on that line, the lives of my kids and myself will never, ever, look the same. This will mark my girls forever. It will set everything into motion. And once started, there may not be a way to stop it. Despite my stubbornness, determination, and desperate grasps and attempts to justify my actions, my heart starts to beat wildly out of my chest. I know I shouldn't do this. Deep down nothing can change that. "Oh God, forgive me for what I am going to do." I know forgiveness doesn't work that way, but in this moment, I hope it does. Shaking, I write my name on that line as neatly as my trembling hand can and pass the papers back to my attorney.

"That's that!" she says. "Let's see . . . today is April third so he should have these within the next couple of days, making it approximately April fifth."

"What did you say today was?" I ask.

"April third—anything wrong?"

"Oh, no. Just curious. Thank you, Dianne." I quickly walk out of the office. April third! How did it end up falling on April third? Today, of all days . . . it's the day I fell in love with Casey, eleven years ago. It's the day we started dating, when I was sixteen years old.

I'm not doing this. Forget it. I'm canceling it. It's signed, yes, but maybe it's not in the system yet. I can still end it. We can stay separated until we find a place of agreement about Tristan. I turn around to go back in and tell Dianne to forget it. Just as my feet hit the brick steps of her office porch, as I begin to walk back in, my phone rings. It's my dad. I break into tears before I can even answer. "Daddy . . ." I say in a broken voice. He immediately speaks before I can say anything else: "My sweet little baby. I knew today would be hard on you. I thought you would need someone to talk to." He continues to speak through my sobbing. "You're doing the right thing." I allow myself to continue to cry as he soothes my rattled nerves. "God sees everything, Lindsey, even the motives of the heart. He sees Casey's crooked nature. He sees his real motives. He sees how he and your mother are throwing you away and intentionally choosing to be blind to the real truth of this situation. They are choosing the ministry over you."

I go ahead and get into my car and drive away. My father stays on the phone with me the whole way home. I cannot wait to be able to move closer to him. That is where I will feel really safe. I know what he is saying is right, what I am doing is right . . . I am right.

Just as I am pulling into Hamilton I receive a text from my mother: "You need to come by my house. Casey thought you might be here so he left you something." I don't respond, but my thoughts immediately run wild—

and, unfortunately for me, so does my heart. "I need to go, Daddy," I say to him. "Casey has left me something at Mom's. I'll call you right back." Fortunately her house is on the way so I swing in. No one is there, but she has left her door unlocked for me. There on her counter sits a stunning vase of my favorite flowers: a dozen roses. The card attached simply reads, "I love you, your husband, Casey." I am utterly speechless. I don't know what to do . . . or think . . . or say. He knew I left to file. Why would he do this? What was his motive? Did he have a motive? I seriously consider throwing them away, but they're so beautiful; and he sent them to me despite the cruelty I showed him. Roses. On April third. I grab them and quickly leave Mom's. I certainly don't want to be here if she were to come in anytime soon—heaven forbid she see the conflicted state I am in right now. It would show me to be weak. And right now, I am weak.

Setting the roses gently in my front seat, I speed back out of her driveway and pick up my phone. "Casey left me flowers, Daddy, a dozen roses. Why would he do that?" I ask.

"You said earlier he left them at your mom's, did you not?" he responds.

"Well, yeah," I reply.

"There's your answer, Lindsey. He knows you moved back in to your first house together. He could have just as easily have had them sent there. But he didn't. He sent them to Karen's so he could make it look to her like he is trying to make things work. This is just so he can keep his job and his place in her ministry. That's his motive. Wow, he really is a sick man! I've never seen anyone so desperate to put on a "Poor me, look how hard I am trying" show. What a fool. Hey, Joyce! Come here, you won't believe what Casey has done now!" I listen as he explains everything to his wife. I can hear her laughing in the background, both of them mocking his gift. I carefully take them out of my car and walk into my house. He returns to our conversation. "Throw them out, Linds. Show them you're not an idiot and that you can see straight through their plans."

"You are right. I'm not going to keep them," I respond as I set them on my kitchen counter, knowing I have no intention of throwing them away. "Well, I just got home. I'm gonna make me some dinner and call it a night. Love you."

"Love you, too, baby girl."

I stand back and admire my gift . . . wishing I didn't love it so much. Wishing it didn't convict every part of what I am doing and, more than anything, wishing it didn't prove my "Casey is cruel, controlling, and abusive" story wrong. But it does. He is none of those things. I convince myself he will change by the time he is served the papers, or maybe when he sees all I have accused him of and lies I have told.

The girls are with him tonight. I will have to find a way to distract my thoughts. I hate being alone now.

The dark voice continually torments me. I have constant conflicting thoughts telling me to stay, telling me to go, telling me I'm right, telling me I'm wrong. The guilt and conviction weighing on my heart and mind forces me to turn to music, movies, books, anything to get my mind of the decision I am making. I decide to turn in early after dinner. But between the meeting I had with Casey this morning, filing the divorce papers with Dianne and now the roses from Casey, sleep eludes me. There are too many thoughts racking my brain. Because of this I go to my most reliable escape plan, the one I have had since I was a little girl; the one I ran to every time I felt pressure to change, every time I was faced with any form of trauma or stress, every time I was told to grow up. I grab the DVD sitting on my entertainment center and pop it in: *Peter Pan*. I begin to reminisce about the first time I tried to escape to Neverland. I wonder if it hasn't played a part in my desperate attempts to escape today. As the movie begins to play, I doze off and dream of that first night I tried to fly away . . . many, many years ago.

Chapter 7

LOST GIRL

Lauren and I curl up as close as we can as our TV casts shadows onto our wall. My sister is three years older than I, and though we are blood siblings, we look little alike. Her blonde hair and porcelain skin are a stark contrast to my almost black tresses and freckled cheeks. She is so beautiful, like a doll you see in a toy store, and far braver and stronger than I am.

It is well past our bedtime, but we beg our mother to let us watch *Peter Pan* one more time. With our family having been torn apart and our lives in an upheaval, it seems to be the only thing that takes us away from the pain and calms us inwardly enough to sleep.

Mom rewinds the video cassette and pushes play. She prays for us, kisses us goodnight, tucks us in tight, and leaves us to take that wonderful journey to Neverland again. Although I have seen *Peter Pan* enough times to quote it, this time is different. Maybe it is mommy and daddy's divorce that causes Wendy's famous question to repeatedly ring through my mind: "But Peter, how do we get to Neverland?" Peter replies joyfully, "Fly, of course!" The statement suddenly takes deep root in my eight-year-old heart. Fly. Oh, to be able to fly! To be able to escape this ugly, painful world, to be able to soar past the stars to a beautiful island where you never have to worry about grown-up things again. But how do I fly? My child-like wondering begins to spin out of control. How can I fly to Neverland? I know I'm not a very fast runner at school, or good at any sport for that matter, but I am sure I could fly pretty well. On the screen, Peter answers my question as quickly as it crosses my mind. "Oh it's easy! You think of a wonderful thought."

That's it? Wonderful thoughts? Oh, I can do that! I will think the most wonderful thought ever! Then Peter will come for me. Then I can fly! I feel excitement and hope starting to rise within me. I don't know why I have never thought about this before! Peter can come for me, too! I'll see his shadow in my house, and I'll run away and never have to feel all these painful feelings again. I'll never have to worry about grown-up things like divorces again! I'll never have to feel the pain of not feeling wanted by Daddy when we go to visit him. I'll never have to hear Momma cry ever again. I'll never have anyone hurt my feelings. I can be free and happy! I really can! I will have to find a way to bring my sister, of course, and my dog. But Peter will let me. He let Wendy take her brothers.

Ok. Wonderful thoughts. Happy thoughts. I close my

eyes and think with my young mind every happy thought I can muster. I try to remember tractor rides with my grandpa Papaw Bill, go-kart cruising with my best friend Ashley, my golden retriever Lady chasing me through our large front yard. But none of it comes to mind. The only real picture I have managed to pull up is one of my daddy, and it isn't a happy thought.

In my mind I see the most important man in my world sitting by the front door in the old, green chair. He has his suitcase beside him and he is crying. He says he's going away. I don't understand. Mommy is a singer and she and Daddy always went on trips, but they always came back. Why isn't she going with him this time? Does he have a trip all by himself? And why does it feel like, this time, he might not come back? What will happen to Lauren and me if he doesn't come back? What will happen to my room? Will we not have anywhere to live anymore? Where will we go? Will I not have a daddy? What will happen to Mommy? She will be sad and I don't like it when she is sad. Did I do something wrong? Did I make him mad again? I really try to be good and not get in trouble, but sometimes I can't help myself. Sometimes I disobey and am bad. Would that make him want to leave? Did he find another little girl he likes more than me, and Lauren? Does he want her to be his daughter instead?

"I promise I will be better if it will make you stay, Daddy," I desperately want to say. "I'll be nice to my sister,

I'll clean my room, I will do anything you ask me to do. I'll be a good girl, Daddy, I promise. I'll be really, really good." But the words never come out. "Why couldn't you have just said you're sorry, Daddy, and then we'd have lived happily ever after? That's what you teach Lauren and me, to always say sorry and move on from it. So why can't you do the same? I don't care if it is something you did, Daddy! If for no other reason, fix it for me! I love you both! Can't you put the papers away for the love of your two daughters? Do you not know how much Lauren and I love you, Daddy? We don't understand. Why, *why*, when I didn't make this choice, why am I the one bearing the consequences of it? Why do I have to suffer for it? *It is your fault*, not mine! I didn't do anything wrong, but I love you and ask you to love me back. Was that so wrong? Did I ask too much? This choice should be on you, Dad, not me. It should hurt you, not me. You should have to pay for this, NOT ME! Who chose this life? Who decided a family ripped apart would be the best option? And whoever it was, un-choose it. Make another choice. I don't care what excuse you give. This didn't have to happen. We could have been a family. You should live with the consequence of that choice, but you don't. I do. I am the one watching it all fall apart. And it is falling down on me." Not a word of it leaves my mouth. All the questions, the pain, the unknowing, it all goes unsaid. I am frozen, looking into the blue-green eyes of my daddy.

With tears streaming down his face he hugs me and says

goodbye. I am left standing by the front door without him. I don't realize the next time I see him he will be living somewhere else, and will be a completely different man to the one I've known. When he pulls out of the driveway, I don't realize I will spend the next decade traveling every other weekend back and forth between houses, cities, and states. I don't realize there will be another woman at dinners with us when we go to see him. When I go to bed that night without Daddy, I don't know about the decisions and consequences I myself will later make as a result of living in a broken home.

Standing by that closed door I knew something was very different. A strange darkness had started to take over my home: a dark cloud of instability. Fear. Terrible sadness. I remember not being able to sleep well that night. I remember seeing terrible, ugly, animal-like creatures with bright green eyes sitting on the dresser in the bedroom. They looked like hyenas, but darker and evil. They turned their heads and stared at me. I blinked hard, wanting them to go away, but they didn't. They stayed. Watching me. I wanted Daddy to come in and make them go away. But he was not there.

I remember visiting Daddy at his new house for the first time. He was sad—sad and very distant. Like he didn't really want us there. Like he wanted to be left alone in his own dark cloud. It seems this horrible, depressing presence is following us everywhere. I wanted him to play with us again. I wanted to see him laugh again. I wanted him to pick me up and hold me close and tell me how much he loves me and that everything will be ok. But none of it happened. Because it was not ok. None of it was ok.

I manage to untangle myself out of my depressing thoughts and look back to the screen. I am expecting to see Wendy taking off for Neverland. To my terrible surprise, I see the credits rolling and hear the lyrics that signal the end of the trip to that magnificent island: "Think of all the joy you'll find, when you leave the world behind and bid your cares goodbye. You can fly, you can fly, you can fly!"

NO! No, no, no! The movie is over. I can feel the excitement that I had felt as the movie began start to die down as panic takes over my mind. "Oh, please, play it again! Please! *Please!*" I think to myself. But it's too late now. I missed it. I missed Peter Pan coming for me. My stupid imagination got away from me. I didn't get to leave my world behind. All my cares and troubles are still here! It's my fault. I had no good thoughts for Peter to come and teach me how to fly. He couldn't come for me. You can't have bad thoughts and still expect to fly.

Lauren is sleeping peacefully beside me. Even though I am fairly certain I have missed my chance for escape, I try to stay awake and look desperately for any sign of Pan's potential coming. How I desperately hope he is coming for me. I mean, I know my happy thoughts are not the best, or, really, not even happy at all, but maybe he can still come. He will understand what is going on with our family. Maybe he can teach me how to have happy thoughts! Or, even better, maybe he has some happy thoughts he can share with me. I'm very good at sharing, and I know he will be too. I listen for the sound of his fairy, Tinker Bell. If I can't get a happy enough thought maybe she will have enough pixie dust to get me there. I turn my ear to the silent room, listening for a sound. Any sound. But there is nothing, no sound at all—at least, not yet. I search desperately for a shadow. There is none. Maybe just a little longer . . .

It's getting later and later. I reason that Peter is having a hard time finding our house. It will just be a little later than I thought, but he'll come. I begin to doze off and imagine swimming with the mermaids, sword fighting with pirates and dancing next to the Indians around a great, warm campfire.

I can't keep my eyes open any longer. I'm sure he will come for me while I am asleep. Then, when I wake up, I'll be in Neverland. Unable to stay awake for another minute I give up my search for Peter and hold on to the hope that somehow I can still make it there by morning. "Goodnight, Neverland," I whisper, "I'll see you soon."

I wake abruptly from my horrible dream. I am back in the living room of my house with the DVD menu of Peter Pan playing repeatedly. I fell asleep again, like I always used to when I was a little girl, and Pan still hasn't come for me. I glance at my phone to see the time: it is mid morning! I jump up and rush to get ready. It is Friday—

rehearsal day. Though there is nothing to rehearse, I still try to go and practice anyway, if for no other reason than to just stay in shape, since I am no longer dancing full time at the ministry. I have to stay up to par if I am ever to have my dream dance career one day.

Tristan and I used to use these days to prepare him for his audition for a short Disney internship. In the past month he has occasionally stopped in to train on his own, too, since he can no longer work with me. I am never there when he is, though—it's just too risky to get caught and there are enough rumors as it is. Though I have not spoken to him in well over a month, I am hoping he'll happen to show up anyway. I miss the world we created. I miss our own Neverland.

Chapter 8

GOODNIGHT NEVERLAND

I quickly realized after that first night searching and waiting to go to Neverland as a child that life doesn't deal out beautiful fantasies without any challenges attached. Days passed, then weeks, months, and years. Peter never came for me. Though we eventually got to the place where we didn't have to watch *Peter Pan* every night, still, many times when I went to sleep, I often found myself frozen by that green chair, looking into the eyes of my daddy, hoping that Neverland was still real. Hoping I would never have to grow up, because growing up hurt.

It's a fantastic notion, isn't it, to never grow up? What a thought: to never have to worry about the responsibilities of life. No bills, no kids pulling on your sleeve, no house to clean, no reality of life trying to eat your dreams alive; it seems as if there would be no worries at all. As hard as it is for some of us to admit it, Neverland is not a place; it's a state of mind. It's the mental and emotional escape from the real world. It is being able to detach oneself from what is in front of them and pulling away to a place where there are no worries. In order to stay in this "Neverland" you have to let go of the thing that is holding you back, the one thing that is keeping you from being young and carefree again. In many ways, the escape mentality has the same effect as a drug. It is used to numb and run from pain. The person escaping carries the same mindset as someone who runs to alcohol as a means of escape. It is the same kind of "need."

There are many means of mental escape. For me it was Peter Pan and Neverland, so it is the example I'll use for this book. Keep in mind as you read, however, the different escape methods you or a loved one is, or has possibly been, using in order to cope with life.

Peter Pan is not bad, nor are most other fairytales. In fact, it remains to this day one of history's greatest pieces of children's literature and an all-round excellent story. However, when a story becomes an escape, a way of thinking that you don't really have to grow up, a way of never changing who you are, then that story becomes deadly to your relationships, marriage, and life. It stunts the growth of a healthy, thriving life and the relationships you should be having in it.

You may be asking, "Oh come on, do people really think they can actually fly away to Neverland?" No, they don't, but here is what they do think and how Neverland plays out in the real world: that friend of yours, the one with the carefree, go-with-the-flow, "you should be enjoying and living differently than how you are living now" attitude, becomes your Peter Pan. They become your way out of your world. Your job, the bar with your newly-found "friend," those few hours hanging out at a game or concert or party, can become your Neverland. I'm not referring to or calling all of those things "escapes." It is when the thought of being able to get away consumes your mind. It is when you begin to continually, over and over and over again, every day, start spending those couple of extra hours at work because you really don't want to go home. People who are called "workaholics" are a good example of how work can be used as a means of escaping. The motivation may be different, but it is a way of avoiding having to face something in life.

When you spend too long in that state of mind and lifestyle you will find that your family, spouse, and kids become more and more of a burden than a blessing. You'll soon find yourself longing for this other fantasy life that has told you, "Come this way and you'll never have to grow up; you can be free and happy here." It will not be long until you are consumed by that world and way of thinking. If never faced and dealt with, you will eventually "fly away with Peter Pan" to Neverland, and you won't come back home. You will lose your way.

It's interesting, isn't it, that in the actual story of Peter Pan, the longer people stay the more they forget about their life back home. They forget they had a family, and their new normal is "running from pirates" which, in the story, also represents growing up. In the original writing by J.M. Barrie, Captain Hook is running from the crocodile, who made a ticking sound after swallowing a clock, which represented an adult running from what was trying to kill him: time. Time is represented by the ticking, the sound Hook feared the most, and the crocodile was always "licking his chops" for Hook because he loved the taste of him so. The message being told is literally, "Run from time, for it will never stop hunting you. Run from growing up because it will kill you." Again, please understand, these stories are amoral; they are neither good nor bad. It is what a person does with the story that makes it destructive or helpful.

What I have found, however, is this "Neverland" mindset that tells you to "Run away, run and you'll never have to worry about grown up things again" is as deadly as poison. In the real world we don't have little green fairies that drink that poison for us. In the real world this poison spreads until it consumes every part of our way of thinking and living.

The world we escape to paints a beautiful fantasy for us and, trust me, it really does look wonderfully appetizing. For those few moments that you get to spend there, life is really great. It is peaceful and happy. You're surrounded by people that "love and understand" you. But that world is a mirage—IT IS NOT REAL! It's the same as when a person is traveling through a desert and can swear they see an oasis up ahead, but when they get there it is a lie, there's nothing there. The fantasy you've created for yourself will leave you empty. Life will catch up with you. You will eventually have to face what you've been running from. On that day you will have to make a choice, but if you choose correctly you will find that reality is so much sweeter than the fantasy. When we fix the problems in our realities, THAT life becomes far more beautiful than anything we could create as an escape. Sound impossible? Trust me, it's not.

Pain, trauma, life—we all handle it differently. For me, I chose that fantasy escape world, and I did it well. I chose to stand in front of my problems and, while facing them, be somewhere else completely, a beautiful place where I would never have to be hurt by anyone or ever feel pressure again. I became very good at detaching myself from growing up. Sure I got older, taller. I married and had kids, but, in my mind, it was the one place only I had access to, the one place I could be young forever.

Everything changed the day I said goodbye to my daddy at that wretched, green chair. That little broken girl froze herself in that moment and never moved past it. My family became just another one of the more than 50 percent of shattered Christian families that day. We became nothing more than another statistic. My home was attacked—not just by a spirit, but by a choice. A *choice* ripped my childhood apart. But whose choice was it? It certainly was not mine. So why am I having to pay for it? This is unfortunately the same fate as countless others. Any trauma like a divorce, a death—anything that causes a significant loss in someone's life—can cause that frozen-type moment. For me, the loss of my security, my hope of a fairytale ending, the loss of my childhood relationship with my father, caused me to stop growing in some ways.

After spending my life trying to escape I found that I couldn't stand to be with people who tried to force me back into reality. I found myself hanging with people who were younger, single, free, and had little-to-no responsibilities of any kind. Keep in mind, however, I was doing this as a married woman with children. I needed to grow up, but I was frozen in time. My mind wouldn't grow up. I consumed myself in a fantasy world, in Disney songs and movies. It was the only thing that kept me happy. I lived for the moments I could "run away" from life and be happy. But those moments were always too short lived. I surrounded myself with friends who would support that way of thinking and those who thought just like me— that it was okay to never grow up.

Chapter 9

TREE AND BIRD

At over six feet tall, Tristan's dark stature towered over my relatively small frame. His dark brown, almost black eyes constantly searched for the magic and fun in the world. He was Peter Pan, and I was Tinker Bell. Together we created a beautiful dream world into which few others were ever allowed.

In that fantasy world, anything was possible. We dreamed as big as we wanted and no one could tell us it wasn't real. And did we ever dream! In our world there were no worries, no responsibilities.

We created an empire for that world—a dance, theater, and music empire that would one day hold hundreds of students and performers alike. We knew we could do it as long as we did it together. Tristan told me I had what it took to be a top-notch director and that no one should hold me back or make me feel like it couldn't or shouldn't be done. To him, I was the best of the best. We dreamed up things like a monstrous theater with red seats, sparkling gold trim and a pit to hold a full-scale orchestra. We dreamed of a school that would have classes for every dance genre you could think of, with each classroom being decorated to fit the look of that particular dance style. The music room would have walls of instruments as well as large areas with computers, DJ, and composition equipment. The dance rooms would have towering floor-to-ceiling mirrors, with grand pianos and custom floors. We would have a theater school, costume departments, and hair and makeup programs. We would have a company for handicapped people who always wanted to dance or sing or act but never had the chance to.

We spent nearly every day together, sometimes planning what we could do with our own company one day and sometimes working on our usual day-to-day responsibilities of what needed to be done for our current job's next event or upcoming production. Writing, dreaming, and dancing—it was a never-ending cycle where we found our own Neverland. We would forget the dreary world outside, and wherever we were became filled with magic and wonder. Here, the world was ours and we could be anything. We had our nicknames, our movie quotes, our songs, our countless lists of inside jokes that only we could understand. We talked from across rooms with nothing more than a glance. We glided together with perfect motion, smooth as silk, across the dance floor. He never faltered, I never fell. I was safe. I trusted him completely. We compared ourselves to the great dance partners of the world, believing that probably none of them had the connection we had.

We danced and the outside world didn't exist, and after that there was no going back. Though nothing ever became physical in our relationship, or even romantic for that matter, we still had a deep connection that I didn't have with anyone else. Tristan was my very best friend. Some could say I made him my "soul mate," someone to whom I had bound my mind, my emotions, and my will. He was the one person I could say anything in the world to and who could equally confide in me, the one person I thought knew me the most. The real problem was, he was not my husband. Instead, he took my husband's place. To be honest, I never intended to get to know him in the way that I did. But those relationships are never intentional. And now it's too late.

After working together for four years, partnering together, writing five theatrical productions, three recitals, well over fifty pieces of choreography, running a dance school, and choreographing, teaching, traveling with, and managing the ministry team *Chosen*, it's not hard to see how a deeply emotional friendship formed. But now it is all crashing down.

Walking into the mirror room of the local gym where we usually practiced I wait, hoping Tristan will show up. It's the rehearsal space we come to when we don't want to be bothered or seen. Before my world started caving in Tree was planning to audition for a short internship at Disney. I am hoping I can hear how it went, be able to tell him about the recent events transpiring between me and Casey, maybe even discuss the future of our own company. Maybe now that papers have been filed, Tristan and I can start acting on all those dreams and plans, even though it may take a little longer than expected. It's been so long since we last spoke. We've never gone more than a day without talking and month is more than I can stand. Finally the door opens. My heart sinks. It's not him.

Ashley Freeman is looking at me from the doorway. She frequently comes to help me train. She is one of my best friends and our best dancer. I met her and her husband, Josh, a couple of years ago when they came to be a part of the Ramp's ministry school, and she joined the performing arts program Tristan and I ran. We have remarkably similar stories, except hers had a happy ending. Although she was never for me and Casey separating, or for me filing for the divorce, she's remained one of the few people I still have in my life. Even so, I didn't even tell her I filed until after I had done it. Despite her remarkably slender and less than five-foot frame she is notorious for her fiery, passionate personality, as well as speaking her mind—and she speaks it brutally so! She's one of those people who will tell the truth regardless of whether or not you want to hear it. I knew she would have told me exactly what I should really have done instead.

Before I can say anything to her, she walks over to me and speaks. "He's not coming, Linds. You know that." I start to tear up and look over at her. "You've got to stop this foolish life you're trying to live in and think about what is really important at this point," she says to me.

There she goes with her brutal honesty, and now it's making me angry. I want her to side with me, to stay in my fantasy world with me.

"Have you heard from Tristan at all?" I ask her.

"Yes, we have," she replies. "He left town today. He's going back home."

Going back home? What does she mean? He's left town? I can't believe it. He was supposed to stay with me. I turn to face her, "And how exactly would you know that?"

"He came by the house earlier this morning." I look at her, furious, as she tells me everything that happened.

"He had already made up his mind to go back home, Lindsey. He made it up weeks ago. Especially now that he doesn't have a job, and probably wouldn't find anything decent here. Truth be told, he lost his job because of the relationship you two had. He needed advice on what to do concerning him and you, and you and Casey, and what he needed to do now. Josh told him to leave the two of you alone, to let you restore your marriage, and to stay out of it."

I stare at her blankly as she continues telling me about the rest of his visit. I am furious at both her and Josh. I am furious at Tristan. Why didn't they tell me he had been at their house? I could have found some way to sneak over and at least have said goodbye to him. Now it's too late, and I may never get the chance again.

Our partnering days are over. The connection we had is gone forever. The friendship is nothing now. The dream I created with him is gone. I so wish it were not true, but it is. What will I do now? I can honestly say I never intended for our relationship to turn into what it did. I can honestly say, even now, I never intended for it to ever have become romantic in the future. I just wanted to be able to have everything I dreamed of for my own life, and for both he and Casey to be a part of it. I wanted to keep them both, but now I've lost them both. I wanted Casey to accept the fact that Tristan was an important part of my life too, that I needed him in order to do everything I dreamed of. I can't believe it's all over.

She can sense my anger and hurt, but continues anyway. "He may not ever speak to you again, Lindsey. He's not going to continue to be the cause of a broken marriage. You're going to have to leave it alone and let him go," she says.

That's far easier said than done. Just let him go? I've already lost Casey; now I've officially lost Tristan. Even the work meetings we had in secret are gone. If nothing else we could have gotten together and worked on dances, just for the sake of being creative, just for the sake of doing something . . . anything . . . just so we wouldn't totally lose each other. But we have. Peter Pan is gone, and I'm a Lost Girl again.

I want to blame Tristan for everything, for the loss of my dreams. Now everything is going to have to change and I'll have to figure out some other way to make my dreams happen. I want to blame him for the loss of my marriage. It would be so easy to cover my tracks and say, "He lured me away from my husband," but I know that would not be the truth. Had I not lied to him, too, and presented Casey in such a negative light we never would have gotten into the relationship we had. I could have protected and shielded my marriage. But I didn't. I knew my husband would never support a career that had already consumed my mind and life, much less allow me to have a career with another man who has taken his place in my heart.

Ashley touches my arm and snaps me out of my thoughts. "I know you're mad at me, and quite frankly I don't care. I know what this path will cost you, Lindsey, and it is not worth it." I say nothing to her but still she continues. "How can you do this when you saw what my situation almost cost me?" she asks.

"I'm not you, Ashley. You know what I went through is totally different."

"Oh, I know. I know everything, Lindsey. Or did you forget that, too? As much as you may want me to, I don't just see one side. You can lie to everyone else but I've seen the way you and Tristan look at each other in rehearsals, so you can't lie to me. You're not the person I have known these past couple of years. You've changed and it's not for the better. You're going to lose everything, including yourself, and when that happens you may not have anyone there to help you pick up the pieces. So, take it from someone that loves you—get a grip, and fix this."

I turn sharply from her, grab my things and walk out. I know I won't stay mad at her forever, but now my day is ruined by the knowledge that I've lost Tristan. My dreams? They're gone. He's gone. He was supposed to be there at the end of this. We even talked about what life would begin to look like when the marriage ran its course. I need to talk to him, to vent to him, to see where I am supposed to go from here. But I can't, and I know my last chance to do this is gone forever.

My heart is shattered. I am losing everything, and though I figured we would have to back off from each other for a while, I never expected to lose Tristan completely. He was one of the main reasons I was doing this. He had to know that, and now he has dropped me. He said he would never leave, that he would stand with me through this, but he left. He's gone. I am alone. Dumped. He was supposed to be there for me, but he tucked tail and bailed, leaving me to deal with the damage. I can't stay here. I have to get out . . . tonight.

Chapter 10

VOICES

One of the things I found most shocking about my journey was how quickly my circle of friends changed when I started taking the road of offense and bitterness. Suddenly I found myself connected to people who were also offended and bitter. Their situation didn't have to be exactly like mine. The offense was the same.

The enemy will always see to it that you are surrounded by people who will agree with you and support you in your cause. It is just what 1 Corinthians 15:33 (NKJV) says, "Do not be deceived: evil company corrupts good habits." When truth comes to you and you seek counsel, those friends will always be the ones to urge you back on the "right" path.

The people I found myself around were the ones who supported my "I don't want to grow up, I want to be free and happy" mindset. They never put me under pressure of any kind. They took all the pressure off of me. I could act how I wanted, be who I wanted. I never had to grow or change. For me, escaping into my fantasy world was exactly what the enemy could use to lure me away from my marriage and ultimately my walk with God. So the people he put in my path were people just like me. Some were married, going through their own divorces—supporting me in my "faultless" divorce and I supporting them in theirs, backing my every accusation of Casey being abusive and controlling. It didn't matter if the accusations were true or not. The most important thing was getting out of the marriage and being happy. Other people were simply offended: offended at the ministry, offended at Casey. Offended friends never try to help each other grow. The vast majority, or even the entirety, of the relationship is spent talking about how much we have been wronged and how terrible the other people are. We may even go so far as to pray for the people we are offended at, believing for God to change their hearts. The last group were the single people, the ones who were still free and happy. Here is where I spent most of my time. For me, this group was where the most damage was done. Here I saw what my life could look like if I weren't tied down to the responsibilities of a marriage. They could go out whenever they wanted. They didn't have to be home at a certain time. The world was theirs, and that is exactly what I wanted my life to look like. These were also the people I made my best friends, and the ones I began to unintentionally model my own behaviors after.

The enemy will also use a "best friend" of the opposite

sex to step in and befriend you. Nothing bad at first—it usually starts with a "Hey! How is your day going?" as you pass each other at church or work. Then a friendship is formed when you begin to spend focused time with that person. Don't forget, it is "just as good friends," but that is exactly where the danger begins.

You never intend for affairs to happen. You never see them coming, even. By the time you realize you are in an emotional affair, you are so emotionally involved that you don't want out. It is the church's way of having an affair without having an "affair." Rarely are adulterous friendships or full-blown relationships intentional. Very rarely, especially in the church. But they do happen and, sadly, most of them are not even spoken of. Most people living in adultery don't even think they are in an affair. After all, they've not had sex, right? They probably haven't kissed, or even held hands for that matter! But their hearts are gone from their spouse, and they are longing to spend their time with another. They dress in ways the other person finds attractive. They talk like them, act like them, talk about them constantly, are seen with them everywhere they go. You don't have to have sex to commit adultery. If you are hiding and deleting text messages, you are already there. This is the emotional affair.

Matthew 5:27-28 says, "You have heard the command-ment that says, 'You must not commit adultery.' But I say, anyone who even looks at a woman with lust has already committed adultery with her in his heart." Many do not believe an emotional affair exists. I used to be one of them—until I had one. I was someone who read that verse and thought things like, "That is in no way referring to my situation. For one, Jesus is speaking primarily to men because, for the most part, they're more susceptible to lust than women, aren't they; for another, I am not lusting after this friend of mine." Okay, let's just be real here. This verse applies to all—men *and* women. We have to stop reading things exactly how we want so that we don't have to apply it to our lives. Lust happens when we desire with our eyes something we want but don't or can't have.

You don't have to verbally share deep romantic feelings with that person to be in an emotional affair. Actually, you don't have to share feelings for each other at all. You just have to have the feelings present, and usually, words do not need to be spoken, nor are they. In your heart, both of you know how you feel, no need to admit it out loud—because if you do, now you're in sin, now there is an admission to the feelings. But to keep quiet and go about living in the feelings silently, now we can justify the actions. If there is an unwillingness to cut off a relationship or friendship, a defensiveness to it, that is the answer to whether or not an affair exists. And that answer is yes. There should be no friendship we would not be willing to immediately sever if it made our spouses feel uncomfortable. If we are unwilling to do so, we must check out hearts and know that the tug we feel to keep someone on the side or in the place of our spouse is all the more reason to cut it off.

If, while you are reading this chapter, a certain "friend" of yours keeps coming to mind, check your heart. It is probably someone the Lord is flashing lights at you for and telling you to stop before it is too late.

Emotional affairs usually happen when there is a need in one person that they believe is not being met by their spouse. The problem is that need is most likely not even supposed to be met by them and is something the Lord is trying to fill. When it is an issue between the two married parties, instead of it being discussed and fought through as a couple, one of them will begin to shut him or herself away. They'll begin to close the door to their husband or wife. There is an offense in their heart toward them. Suddenly you will begin to take closer notice to this other person you've probably already been friends with, wanting to be around them more, see them more, talk to them more; it's probably someone even your spouse knows. It will very likely be someone you work with. You never mean to have the conversations with them about your husband or wife or the trouble in your marriage, but little by little those conversations happen. The conversation that sparked my own went something like this . . .

Chapter 11
OPEN DOORS

"Hey, Linds. I know it's none of my business, but is something going on between you and Casey? You always seem tense and upset when he comes by rehearsals, and are usually crying when he leaves."

"Everything is fine, Tristan. I'm fine."

"Lindsey, come on. You're crying now."

I erupt in frustration and anger. "He doesn't like me doing this job! He says it consumes me, that the girls need me to be at home more and they are upset when I am not there to say goodnight to them. He says all I do while here or at home is listen to music for choreography, and that I'm disconnected from him and my family. He doesn't understand the demands this job places on me. He has no idea about the deadlines I am supposed to meet or the people that are here who are taking time off from their own jobs to be a part of this. He expects me to just drop it and go home. He thinks it's inappropriate when a twenty-five-year-old woman is dancing on a ministry team with a bunch of teenagers. I'm the lead in every piece we have! It would take months to reconfigure every dance to replace me, besides the fact that I feel this is what I am called by God to do! Any ministry is going to consume your mind to some degree. Of course I am at home working on dances, choreography, technique, and classes. How could I get everything done if I'm not doing that?"

"So, what does he expect you to do exactly?"

"He says it's not about the hours or days I am here, and he wouldn't care so much if I prioritized being a wife and mom first, and also developed friendships with people more in my stage of life and not a bunch of single teenagers. When I am home, he wants me to be fully home, not just there in body but completely gone in mind and heart. He said if I would do that then he could celebrate what I did because it wouldn't be stealing me from him and the girls. He wants to see my focus be our children and our marriage above anything else, that if they really needed me I would be there. If I thought they had a dire need I would absolutely be there! But wanting your wife to be home just so she can sit beside you on the couch while we eat together and watch a TV show is not dire! He doesn't need me there! He wants me to be there just because he wants a 'Stepford Wife,' and I am never going to be that for him! Maybe he just doesn't want me? He doesn't want me. I am never going to be what he wants. He made a mistake choosing me."

"Lindsey, you are no mistake. You are talented and

gifted at this job. It is not right for anyone to make you feel like you're not enough, even your spouse. It's not my business, but what you're going through isn't right. Look at my parents! My mom can do ministry stuff and my dad never says a word about it, because he's completely with her. He's behind her. He believes in her. Look at your own mother. She runs a major worldwide ministry! How could you not have this in your genes? He's the one making a mistake to think you are not supposed to be doing this full-time. No one can change who you are. You're quirky and funny. People adore you. You love everyone and have an uncanny ability to bring out the best in everybody. You pull them out of their box. You are touchable. He is not. To be honest, most people can't stand him. They think he is stuck up and arrogant, and that he thinks he is better than everyone. But you have never been that way. You open your heart to everybody. It is his loss if he chooses not to see that. I know you well enough to know you will not want people to see you upset and start wondering what's wrong. You're too strong for that. I'll have someone get you a coffee, since it always makes you feel better. I'll get rehearsal going. Come out and take over when you're ready."

Little by little these conversations grew deeper and deeper. Arguments between Casey and I got more and more exaggerated as I shared them with Tristan. He became more and more of a comfort for me. Soon it was not just arguments and problems at home I went to him for. He became my very best friend. We eventually ended up talking mostly about his school and classes, and what his family was up to. I became very close to his brother. His brother began calling me his "big sister." His sisters and I became close. I began to pull into his whole family. We Snapchatted constantly, sending funny pics of ourselves back and forth. Nothing was ever, ever inappropriate. Nothing was ever scandalous. In fact, it was the complete opposite. It was usually pictures of me without makeup on, having just woken up in the morning, about to leave for a rehearsal, with a caption saying something like, "Woah . . . Mornings . . . need coffee . . . now." Tristan became someone I was never under any pressure with. In fact, he was the person that took all the pressure off of me. He became very protective of me. He listened to me. He supported every dream I had. He respected me in front of all of our students, got me water before I could even ask for it, would walk in with coffee and always knew my favorite kind, down to the temperature I liked it at. He knew my favorite foods and snacks. When I was caught up and busy with a rehearsal he would frequently have my assistant go get me something to eat, knowing I would probably get so into teaching I would forget to take a break for myself and eat something. He quite literally took it upon himself to see to all of my needs.

It is easy to justify his actions and call them innocent, saying, "Come on, Lindsey, he was just being a good friend." Perhaps. But being a best friend of the opposite sex to a married woman is NOT being a good friend. If someone is showing kindness and thoughtfulness as a friend to another single friend it is wonderful, and they'll probably be someone you want around you all the time. But when someone other than the spouse is meeting the emotional or physical needs of a married person, disaster is most assuredly going to follow.

Let me be absolutely clear about this: your husband or wife is the ONLY person who should be seeing to your emotional and physical needs, the only one with whom you should share your marital hurts with. DO NOT EVER TALK ABOUT YOUR SPOUSE NEGATIVELY TO ANYONE. NEVER! It opens up the door for them to always fail. They will never do or be enough for you. They will always fall short if you are constantly looking for them to mess up. And, when you are constantly running your mouth about them to others, you will always be looking for their flaws.

Is it wrong for a secretary or assistant to see to it you have a meal when you are too busy at a job? Of course it isn't, but there is a fine line between whether or not they are seeing to a part of your job, or meeting a need you have inside of you.

Your relationship with your husband or wife is like an open window. When you are completely open to them, all other windows are shut. There is free-flowing love and communication constantly. But that window works like a scale of sorts. If you ever crack a window somewhere else, the one to your spouse closes a little. Texting or calling someone of the opposite sex just to talk because you enjoy their company more than your spouse? The window closes some. Having coffee during work breaks together regularly? The window closes some more. Eventually you will find yourself with a window that is completely closed off to your spouse and wide open to another. Now you probably don't even want to reverse it and, if you ever find yourself wanting to, it may be too tightly shut. ✳

You never realize something like an emotional affair is happening. You are very careful to guard your heart and to prevent things like that. But still, an open window to a casual friend can quickly turn into something never intended. By the time you realize what is happening, you don't want out. Now you are involved. Now the excuses start for why you are staying at work a little later, why you have to go in on your day off. You do things like change the passcode on your phone, and change all your social media passwords. You and the other person will even make excuses to each other as to why you're meeting for no reason whatsoever. You will attempt to justify it even to yourselves.

What do you do if you find yourself in this relationship? Even if you did want to get out, how do you? Well, let's look at the two options. On one hand, you can keep the affair. You'll have the excitement and the fun and the magic of something new. You'll have someone you think agrees with you and believes in you. Someone who is easy to talk to, who likes what you like, and you have so much in common with. However, this relationship, though easy to try to justify, will never line up with the Word or will of God, and God will not bless a relationship birthed out of sin. The other option is to cut the relationship off, block them from every part of your life, and invest the same kind of commitment and love that you've been investing into this other person back into your spouse. You can still have the excitement and the fun and the magic. You will have someone that agrees with you and believes in you. Only now, it will be right, it will be according to the Word of God. It will have every part of what you're looking for in another while being based out of a depth of love that has stood through trials and still made it. It will be backed by His grace and blessing. If you invest into your covenant relationship the same effort, time, and affection that you have been putting into the affair then you and your spouse will have everything you've ever dreamed a relationship could be, and so much more.

The saying goes: "The grass is greener on the other side." Actually, grass is green where you water and nurture it. To cut off the extramarital relationship is going to hurt. I mean, you never talk to them again. NEVER again. You will lose them forever. Everything you are looking for in another is to be found in your spouse. If it were not so you would never have married them in the first place. To sever the affair and restore the marriage will be hard, because the truth of the matter is there are real feelings there and feelings hurt. But what you will gain from choosing your spouse over everyone else is far beyond measure.

Choose love. True, real, godly love.

Chapter 12

NASHVILLE

I storm out of the gym and think quickly of where I can go tonight. Tupelo, the next town over, is a decent get-away; plenty of good restaurants but not nearly enough cover. Too many Ramp students work there, though, and I am in desperate need of a drink. Heaven knows what would be said if any of them caught me drinking. I pace around for a while in the packed parking lot. Hopefully no one in this lot is connected directly to The Ramp or mom, but you never know. To hide anything I do I will have to get far away. Finally, it dawns on me—I pick up my phone and call Ava, a long-time friend of mine who lives a few of hours east of here. Since Casey has the girls for a couple more nights, maybe I can escape for a little while. I can't stand to be here any longer and it's still early enough in the day to make a short trip, as long as I can keep it secret that is. I'm in too much of a haste to check my surroundings for prying ears.

"Lindsey! I haven't heard from you in a long time. What's

going on? Are you okay?" she asks when she answers her phone.

"No. I'm not. I'll explain later. Listen, I know it's last minute but can I crash at your place for a couple of days? I have to get out and go . . . somewhere."

"Of course, girl! I'd be thrilled! Mom will want to see you, too."

"Thank you so much. I'll be there in a few hours."

I quickly rush home, throw my things in a bag and drive the three and a half hours to her house. Before I unload my things I see Ava walking outside to meet me. Something is wrong, but I can't quite figure out what it is. I walk up and meet her in her driveway.

"Don't come in yet," she says. "Your mom called. She's on the phone with my mom right now."

What! How did she know? I told no one! Ears: they are everywhere. I was so sure there was no one around I recognized when I called Ava. I am so stunned and livid that I automatically begin shaking. I can't believe my mother's nerve, her determination to ruin my life, her will to hunt me down no matter what I do. It's never going to end. Even If I moved to another continent, she would find me, haunting me like a dark shadow.

"What do you need, Linds? How can I help?" Ava asks.

"Take me to a bar." I demand. "And make sure it's one where NO ONE knows who I, my mother, or the Ramp is."

Ava pulls out and begins to speak. I interrupt her before she can. "How does this happen, Ava? Is your family going to turn against me too? Why is my mom everywhere I go? I can't get away from anyone!" I yell ferociously.

"You're an adult woman, Lindsey! Who cares if they know where you go or what you do! And don't worry, my mom is not going to care what you do. And before you ruin both our evenings with paranoia, she's not going to rat you out for going drinking tonight, either. She would probably join us if she could."

"Not caring is far easier said than done. I just want to get away," I say desperately. "I want them to leave me alone. I want to be alone. I don't want to feel any of this anymore! I'll never be free of them, Ava. Never." I wait several moments before I tell her anything about me and Casey. Seeing now how fragile my situation is, and becoming more aware of just how much I am being watched, makes me suddenly very paranoid. "I filed for a divorce. I can't stay in the marriage any longer."

"I already know, Lindsey."

I snap a glance over at her. Is there seriously no one I can trust?

"There are ears and eyes all over that place. I've heard about everything. You've got to start watching your back, especially when it comes to divorce proceedings. The tiniest step in the wrong direction and they will throw it in the papers and try to take everything from you."

She is right. I have been far too careless.

"You know what?" she says. "Forget about all of that for tonight. I am taking you somewhere no one knows who you are or cares about what you do."

I have never had a drink in my life; at least, not for the sake of drinking. When I was a teenager we took communion once while we were overseas and it was actual wine, but other than that I am extremely naive when it comes to alcohol. I don't even know what to order, so I let her do it for me. After two large, mixed rum drinks of some kind I am feeling pretty tipsy and starting to spill my life story to the bartender. Three drinks after that and I remember nothing.

The next morning I wake up in the guest room of Ava's house. There is water and some Advil beside my bed. My head is splitting and I have no idea what happened last night. The thought terrifies me. I stagger into the kitchen where her mother is making coffee.

"Well, good morning, Sunshine!" she says and chuckles. "You had quite the night didn't you?" I say nothing. "Don't worry, I'm not going to say anything to your family. Sometimes you need a night to lose yourself. Besides, it's really none of my business anyway." She passes me a cup of coffee and hugs me. The warmth seeps through the mug to my hands, though I am wishing it could warm the rest of me, but that cold is coming from within. "Get cleaned up if you want. Ava is upstairs. You can just take the day off and do nothing but get away from everything. Tonight we can all have dinner together."

I spend the day doing exactly what she said: nothing. Well, nothing but lying around, drink, get a pedicure, drink, shop some and drink more. I am hoping all the alcohol will at least take me away from all that has been happening, but it doesn't. It makes it worse. I didn't know alcohol could make you drop your guard so much. Now all the defenses I have put up to guard my heart from myself and everything happening around me are down, and I feel everything all at once. Only now I'm feeling it, and I'm also not in control of my body or mind either. What a way to try to get out and bury things for a while!

Over dinner we talk of their jobs and all the great things happening for all of them. Ava is a remarkable singer and is now traveling on her own. Her brother is making great connections as a film producer, her parents are teaching music and writing. Having already succeeded as singers and writers themselves they have no trouble filling up their weekend classes. I envy them; their happiness as a family, their success. And here I sit at their table faking a smile and dying on the inside.

Early the next morning I load up my things to head back home. The girls will be home with me tonight. I need to get home and clean up before they arrive. I am finally sober after a two-day drinking binge, at least I think I am, but I can still feel the grogginess and nausea. It will probably be there for a while, if I had my guess.

"Don't be a stranger, Sweetie!" Ava's mother says, as she hugs me. "Everything will turn out okay, whether you end up with Casey or not."

Ava comes up behind her. "Be careful on your way home. Come back anytime you need to. You are always welcome here."

For the next three hours I drown myself in a CD Ava left with me. She knows music is one of my favorite escapes. Before I make it back to my house I get a message from my mother. "Can you meet me real quick?"

Is she serious? Nothing in me wants to meet with her. I know all we will do is argue about the divorce. Even when our talks don't start out that way, it is always where they end up. She'll never leave me alone if I don't agree to meet, and would probably show up at my house uninvited. I might as well get it over with.

"Fine," I reply back. "Meet me at the Church of God in thirty minutes." I hang up abruptly. Why am I doing this? Why didn't I just say no? What is it in me that still gives in and cowers every time she is around? The last half hour of my trip is now soured. I eventually arrive in Hamilton and pull over into the parking lot of the local Church of God and wait for her to arrive. I'm hoping she won't know why my eyes are so blood shot and why I am so out of it. She pulls in next to me and motions for me to get in to her car with her. I am thankful she notices nothing about the state of my hangover as I hop into her car to talk.

"Lindsey, I don't know why you left or what you did there . . ."

"Ha! Finally I got away with something," I think to myself.

". . . and quite honestly I don't want to know . . ."

"Yes you do, but we'll pretend that statement is true," I think again.

"What I do know is this . . . the decisions you are making are going to completely destroy your life."

If she doesn't know what happened this weekend, what is she talking about exactly? Suddenly it dawns on me: I did not tell her I had actually filed. She knew I had been meeting with the attorney but that was it. I didn't even think to let her know. Casey, or quite possibly the sheriff himself, filled her in. She knows everyone in this town so it could have been anybody. Since I am just sitting and staring at her she continues to speak.

"You are hurting everyone. Me, your sister, Casey. What about the girls? How can you do this after you yourself know exactly what it's like?"

"I'm not trying to hurt anyone, Mom, but if you want to talk about hurt, how about the fact that you have chosen my soon-to-be ex-husband over your own daughter?"

"That is a lie, Lindsey. You know it is a lie. I am not choosing a side with anyone but God and what the Word of God says about your situation. I am not on Casey's side, I am not on yours. I am standing on what is right according to the Word that, deep down, you yourself know is true. Casey is willing to fight for the marriage. He has agreed to go to any counselor, to step down from his position at the ministry, to move away and start over, to do anything to make it work! He loves you, Lindsey! You are the one doing this, not him!"

At that, I erupt. I am so sick of her trying to throw the Bible at me in order to get me to do what she wants. Who is she to say what God wants and is telling me to do?

We stay in the car and go at it for at least another hour. Safe to say, this has not turned out to be the nice little get away weekend I expected it to be. First the meeting with Casey, then filing, then losing Tristan, then losing myself in glass after glass of liquor, now this. After we are both spent and drained I get back in my car and head home. It will not be long before my time starts with the girls for the week so I need to get things together as best I can before they arrive. I can't wait to see them. At least now no one will bother me with them here. If nothing else we all agree that we should try to keep them in the dark as much as possible and not involve them or have them overhear anything. I don't feel like making dinner so I throw a frozen pizza in the oven and pull out some paper and paint for us to play with. I am praying to God the divorce doesn't take long, but somehow I feel this is about to be the war of my life.

Chapter 13

ITCHING EARS

Now the serpent was more crafty (subtle, skilled in deceit)
than any living creature of the field which the LORD God
had made. And the serpent (Satan) said to the woman, "Can
it really be that God has said you shall not eat from any of
the trees of the garden?" And the woman said to the serpent,
"We may eat fruit from the trees of the garden, except the
fruit from the tree which is in the middle of the garden.
God said, 'You shall not eat from it or touch it, otherwise
you will die.'" But the serpent said to the woman, "You will
certainly not die! For God knows that on the day you eat
from it your eyes will be opened [that is, you will have greater
awareness], and you will be like God, knowing [the difference
between] good and evil." And when the woman saw that
the tree was good for food, and that it was delightful to look
at, and a tree to be desired in order to make one wise and
insightful, she took some of its fruit and ate it; and she also
gave some to her husband with her, and he ate.
Genesis 3:1-6, AMP

Since the beginning of time, deception has been the number-one weapon Satan uses against the people of God. It is his greatest and most reliable tactic, for it not only works on the lost, it also works (and actually has most effect) on those who are life-long believers. Deception can so easily take root and grow and we never even know it's there.

Deception works in many different ways and can take several different paths and approaches. It wears many masks and works through things like lies, pride, self-pity, victim mentalities, entitlement mentalities, pain, offense, bitterness, fault casting, or unbelief. The enemy will show you a stunning image of what your life could look like— choices that look like they will have wonderful outcomes, but all of it—ALL OF IT—is a mirage. It is a counterfeit to what is real. If the fruit did not look delicious or, as the verse above states, "delightful to look at," Eve would never have given it a second thought. It was the beauty of the enemy's words and false promises that caused her to give in and take what she thought was lovely and would give her life for. In the end, it cost her everything—a choice with consequences that are still being seen today.

Although deception has no limits to its methods, the following examples of how deceit works, and the paths it can take, are just a few that took hold of my own mind, as well as the mindsets I have seen destroy the lives of so many others.

1. Believing a Lie

If we really think about it, the enemy does not come to us with a direct lie. If he did, we would recognize the danger of it and never take the bait. So the enemy masks the lie as a truth, knowing that if he can get us to believe a lie as truth then he has a way into our lives. Do not think for one second the enemy can't or won't get inside your head and filter the things you hear and believe. He is given access the minute you entertain a thought that is contrary to the will and Word of God. Even with Eve there was just enough truth in the serpent's statement to lure her in and cause her to believe that what he said could be taken in as truth. Even more amazing is how Eve already knew the real truth and even repeated it back to the serpent.

Satan knows you would not be swayed if he threw a full-blown lie at you. You would see it coming and be able to easily resist it. But if he can add just one drop of truth to a mountain of a lie, and continue to add another drop at a time to your thoughts, your belief system, then he's done it. And when that ONE thought is accepted and believed then he has you hooked. That thought, though it may contain a sliver of truth, will eventually grow into a full-blown lie, and no small amount of truth mixed with a lie will make it right—it is either all truth or all lie. Truth does not share space with a lie. Eventually, that lie will change who you are. It will permeate every part of your being until you no longer remember what is truth and what is not. All of a sudden you realize you are not at all who you were before and you can't pinpoint how you even got there. Then, at the moment you start to question whether what you are doing and how you are thinking is right or wrong, the enemy will hit you with another deception, backed by just enough truth, mind you, to take you a little deeper. When that deception is questioned he comes with another. The saddest thing is, you have no idea it's happening. You have no idea you are there. You may even believe you are searching for truth and THAT, ALL BY ITSELF, can be the deception: the "Truth Search" deception. What is really dangerous about the truth search is you believe the people you've drawn around you, who say they are trying to help you; and the people who are speaking the REAL truth of the Word of God to you, they're the ones that are really deceived, and you think YOU are the one living the truth.

2. It Can't Happen To Me

Anyone is capable of anything. That can be a positive statement, pushing us to achieve great things, or it can be destructive, causing us to make life-shattering decisions. Some of us have grown up our entire lives in a godly home believing we could never be affected by the enemy, at least not too badly. Some of us were pastor's kids, some had grandmas or a mother or father who prayed and raised us to make wise and godly choices but, even with all that, deception can still take hold; and when it does, its grip is strong, its arm reaches long and it does not let go easily.

No one is exempt from being a target. The minute you think you are immune to Satan's plans is the minute you open the door and make yourself vulnerable. Why do you lock the doors to your house at night? Maybe you even set an alarm that alerts you to any sudden movement in your house. Why do we go to such lengths to have systems that not only alert us but the police, the fire station, and the ambulance? Why do such things? It's to counter the risk of an intruder walking in as they please. We are not so foolish as to leave the doors of our homes wide open to intruders. Not only do the sirens on our alarm systems let us know we are not safe and harm is about to come, they also call for help from a higher authority. If we are so cautious about intruders or burglars for our homes, why then do we leave the doors of our mind and heart wide open to intruders who can breed deception? When it comes to our minds and our hearts, it is easy to go about unprotected because, after all, what real harm can come there?

3. Nothing Will Happen To You

The enemy will always downplay the severity of the consequence of our choices in order to cause us to take the bait. "You won't lose *everything* if you, without cause, file for a divorce; you can still be happy someday. One drink won't ruin your reputation forever. Everyone has a 'one night stand,' it's not that big a deal . . ." It can also come in the subtlest of ways: "The friendship you are in with that man/woman is not an affair. Who said emotional affairs even exist? You are completely justified in having someone of the opposite sex be closer to you than your spouse." Or maybe even, "You are so unhappy and God would want you to be happy more than anything." What he does not tell you is the price you will pay when you accept that way of thinking and believing. It can cost your marriage, your children, your mother and father, your name, your peace of mind, your walk with God, your reputation . . . and it will not just be you who has to pay it. It will also affect those you love and who love you. Thoughts will become beliefs. Beliefs will become our words. Words will become actions. But all of it will begin as a tiny seed planted in our minds.

We often write Satan off as a stupid weakling incapable of doing us any harm because, after all, he is already defeated and can do nothing to us. But even the Word of God says he is "more crafty than any living creature" (Genesis 3:1). Think of a person you know or have heard of to be shrewd and able to sucker and cheat people so they can get whatever it is they want. Have you even been lured into one of these schemes from a sales person, or a friend? Have you been lured into believing something someone said to you, only to be turned away and left broken-hearted? Even the shrewdest and cleverest of these people would still not hold a candle to how easily and perfectly the enemy can deceive.

4. I Can't Be Deceived While I Serve God

Deception is not always a great falling away from the faith. It is not always backsliding. It can also be as simple as living in a lie that you believe to be true. It is so easy to believe that deception looks like someone who falls completely away from the Lord. It is easy to think deception is a complete falling away, that it is walking away from God willingly, intentionally and with both eyes wide open. You never attend church anymore, you never attend family gatherings, you pull away from people you love, you dive headlong into sin, etc. But a life of deception is completely different. The actual dictionary meaning of 'deceive' is "the act or practice of deceiving, concealment or distortion of the truth for the purpose of misleading, duplicity, fraud, cheating; to mislead by a false appearance or statement, delude, to be unfaithful to." When you are deceived, you don't know you are deceived. You can attend church and worship and pray as if NOTHING HAS EVER CHANGED. You teach people the Word, pray with people, pray for people, listen to worship music, read the Word. The danger in this is that you don't know that *you* are the one who believes the lie. Instead, you accuse others of being deceived and blind, and even pray for them to see truth. It is in everyone's nature to want to be right, to believe truth, to see everyone and everything for what it really is. It is in our nature to reject masks, and lies, and false fronts—but the enemy is a master at false fronts. So good, in fact, that we never know it is a mask. We believe the beauty he shows us is real.

Much hinges on what we allow into our minds and hearts. We are fertile soil and the fruit produced in our lives is completely dependent on what seeds we allow in. The tiniest of seeds, though small, can produce a large crop.

The large mustard tree can grow to twenty feet. However, the seed for that tree is no larger than one to two millimeters in diameter. The magnitude of the mustard tree was not due to outside forces. It's potential for size was always in that tiny seed. The truths or lies we believe work in the same way. The crop produced is our choice, and all comes from what seeds we allow to settle in our heart. Seeds of truth or seeds of deception, both will produce.

Chapter 14

DECEPTION

If Satan came and said, "God hates you and wants you to be lonely and in pain," obviously we would not believe it because, as believers, we would start slinging oil, casting devils out, and speaking the Word over our minds. But if he can make you question the will and purpose and goodness of God with statements like, "If God really loved you, why would this be happening? Isn't He all-powerful? Can't He just change your situation and make it go away? He must not be the loving and merciful and kind God you think He is," then a seed of deception can be planted.

How does something like that even begin? As believers who strive to keep our thoughts holy and pure, how do we create ground in our minds that allow those seeds to grow? It usually starts with a pain, offense, or insecurity that we haven't dealt with. The enemy knows where we are weak and could be hit the hardest. For me, I was dealing with the deep underlying pain of a broken family—a situation that, sadly, over half the people alive right now have also come from. So common is a broken beginning that now statements like, "I come from a broken family," are not shocking in the least. I never allowed the Lord to touch the empty place I had been carrying for the entirety of my life. As simple as it sounds, those issues I hadn't dealt with became fertile soil for deception to be planted. Though deception can use life-altering events (the death of a loved one, divorce, church splits, business and financial crashes, etc.), it does not always need one. It can be something as simple as a hurt feeling that takes root as an offense, a statement your spouse made that cut a little deep and was never confronted or dealt with. It could be a family disagreement that turns into bitterness and offense. You can almost always pinpoint the fertile soil by the following: anger, bitterness, un-confronted hurt, insecurity, envy, strife, shame or rebellion. Does it mean you have to be perfect, with no problems ever, in order to be safe? Does it mean you will absolutely, without question, fall prey to deception? No, of course not. It does, however, make you more vulnerable to the effects of deception. 1 Peter 5:8 (AMP) says, "Be sober [well balanced and self-disciplined], be alert and cautious at all times. That enemy of yours, the devil, prowls around like a roaring lion [fiercely hungry], seeking someone to devour." This does not mean we live in fear. It means we live *aware*. It means when an issue comes up, it is dealt with immediately. It means NO PART of us is off-limits to God, NO PART of us is hidden, NO PART of us is untouchable.

Let me show you an example of my own offense and how it worked in my life. During the two years I was away from home, I continued to "serve God," or what I thought was serving God. I would read my Bible and take Bible verses exactly like the one we just read. I would read verses like 1 Peter 5:10 (AMP) that says, "After you have suffered for a little while, the God of all grace [who imparts His blessing and favor], who called you to His own eternal glory in Christ, will Himself complete, confirm, strengthen, and establish you [making you what you ought to be]"; and I would in all honesty and with all my heart believe God was telling me to hold on a little longer because I believed I was being treated wrongly by Casey and my family. I believed He would turn around and bless me for my suffering.

Another verse I frequently read and twisted was Exodus 14:13-14, "But Moses said to the people, 'Don't be afraid. Just stand still and watch the LORD rescue you today. The Egyptians you see today will never be seen again. The LORD himself will fight for you. Just stay calm.'" Is it a powerful verse, meant to give hope in a time of great fear and trial? Absolutely. But when I twisted that verse I began to fight against God. To me Pharaoh represented Casey, my mother, my family. I would literally read the Bible while in full deception and twist Bible verses to make the Word apply to and defend my sin. I would listen to incredible Christian songs that, when sung with a clean heart, open before God, are effective and powerful; but when listened to through the filter of deceit they become just another weapon for the enemy. And yes, Satan will use the Word of God, worship music, even sermons you hear, to try to deceive. In Matthew 4, Satan twisted the Word to Christ Himself, testing Him in one of His weakest moments. Deception will always make you believe you can manipulate the Bible to make His Word support your cause, but no matter how much it is misread and misinterpreted, truth will always, always, always win in the end. His Word will NOT return void, and who knows that just maybe the verse you are trying to twist is the very one that, while you speak it, is altering your future for God's will. I know one thing for sure: although I thought the "Egyptians" I was fighting were people in my life, I have seen the real ones drown. I saw every hurt, every bit of shame, every insecurity, every wrong thought toward my husband and children, every angry, adulterous thought or action, all drown. THAT is the real enemy you are fighting against. Do not let the enemy tell you it is a person, because it is most certainly not. Don't let the enemy make you think you are fighting God. Trust me, God always wins.

Deception makes you believe you can pull the grace and mercy card. It makes us believe and say things like, "I know my situation may not be the *perfect* will of God, but that's what His grace and mercy is for. He knows I am not perfect and am struggling in this area, but He will forgive me. His grace will cover my sin." Grace does not work that way. The price was paid once. ONCE. Jude 1:4 (AMP) says, "For certain people have crept in unnoticed [just as if they were sneaking in by a side door]. They are ungodly persons whose condemnation was predicted long ago, for they **distort the grace of our God** into decadence and immoral freedom [viewing it as an opportunity to do whatever they want], and deny and disown our only Master and Lord, Jesus Christ." *(emphasis mine)*

Grace will not apply to sin when that sin is being done willingly and knowingly while we excuse it under the guise of "grace." Grace applies when we truly see our deception and wretchedness and wrongdoing and come to the Lord in repentance. Grace applies when we stand before a just God, asking forgiveness for our actions, not excusing them. It is when we repent and know we deserve judgment, but instead we are given mercy. THAT is what the cross was for. THAT is what mercy is for. But it will never apply to a person who just wants to be excused of the consequences of their actions.

Deception says we are not wrong. It tells us to point the finger and blame another for our sin. This is also proven in the Garden of Eden at the beginning of time. It is the first initial reaction to deception.

> *But the LORD God called to Adam and said to him, "Where are you?" He said, "I heard the sound of you [walking] in the garden, and I was afraid because I*

> *was naked; so I hid myself." God said, "Who told you*
> *that you were naked? Have you eaten [fruit] from*
> *the tree of which I commanded you not to eat?" And*
> *the man said, "The woman whom You gave to be with*
> *me—she gave me [fruit] from the tree, and I ate it."*
> *Then the LORD God said to the woman, "What is*
> *this that you have done?" And the woman said, "The*
> *serpent beguiled and deceived me, and I ate [from*
> *the forbidden tree]."*
> **Genesis 3:9-13, AMP**

Of course there are many paths the enemy can and will use. He will use whichever one hits closest to home with you. Once you open your mind to the enemy and immerse yourself in deception, the only way you will be able to escape is when the Lord pulls back the curtain and you see the real serpent that has been at work in your life. Deception works by altering, attacking, and changing your core beliefs. It will cause you to question things usually in this order: First the voice of God—those pricks you feel within you, the red flags the Holy Spirit throws up. Then you will question the Word of God—His written Word, the sole truth upon which we base our entire lives. At this stage you will find yourself twisting and manipulating verses to justify sin and wrong choices. Then you will eventually question the sovereignty, the justness, the righteousness or even the existence of God at all. You will find yourself drawn to people who will justify your cause and thoughts. You will mask it by saying, "I am just trying to figure out what the truth REALLY is about God and what the Bible REALLY says about my situation." Those people, who have similar offenses, hurts, and deceits in their own life, will not only justify your newly-found beliefs, they will say things like, "No way! Me too! I have been on that same path to try to find truth." You will be surprised at how eerily similar your stories and interests are. They are looking for truth, and you are looking for truth. But Yahweh God, the God of heaven and earth, would NEVER send someone into your life who would cause you to entertain and question God's holiness, goodness, sovereignty, or truth.

Anyone coming alongside you who justifies or causes you to question ANYTHING contrary to the Word of God has been sent by the same enemy that is at work in their own life. Not only are they in danger of standing before a just God for taking part in helping deceive you, YOU, my friend, are also in danger of standing before that same great Judge for justifying THEIR untruthful and deceitful beliefs back to them. Deception is drawn to deception. Offense is drawn to offense. Look around at the people you are hanging around with. Most likely it is people you have not been friends with for very long. It is people you suddenly got close to just as your situation took a turn for the worse.

Chapter 15

OWEN

Several months have passed. No divorce. We had one mediation in June. We had everything settled. Casey was even going to let me move to where my dad was. But as soon as I told Dad the custody arrangement of week on/week off he took major issue with it.

"That is never going to work, Lindsey! Please tell me you didn't sign anything making that final," Dad says over the phone.

"Nothing has been signed yet. It's just the verbal agreement we have until the attorneys can type up the actual settlement," I reply.

"Honey, that will never work. Those girls will live in the car. Homeschooling would be the only option and there's no way you could do that and still work a job up here to support yourself. You're going to have to call it off."

Needless to say, that arrangement never got signed. Since mediation failed they tried to schedule a court hearing in July, but that didn't work out either due to a scheduling conflict with the judge. So now, here I am . . . waiting. It is late summer now. I had to take a job at a high-end salon in the Florence Mall for the time being. I could have gotten one in my home town, Hamilton, but nothing in me wants to be in this city right now—not unless I had absolutely no other choice. The hour drive to Florence and back every day is pretty grueling but it beats seeing the people I really don't want to see, and hearing all their questions and accusations. Plus, it prevents any confrontation Mom wants to have. However, she has started shopping in the mall I work at a lot more than she used to.

The loneliness is getting pretty difficult to bear now. When the girls are not with me there is nothing to do after work but sit in my house alone. Ashley and Josh check in on me and frequently have me over to their house but, at the end of the day, I still have to come home to nothing. I bought a puppy to at least try to fill the unbearable emptiness, but even with that, at night I am still in bed alone, sometimes fighting off the longing I have to feel Casey's warmth beside me.

My sister and I have lost almost all contact. I don't understand why we could walk together through our own parents' divorce but she abandons me now. Lauren was my hero, my only constant while growing up in a broken home. Now, when I need her more than ever, she is gone. Like everyone else in my family she is completely deceived, blind to what is right in front of her . . . her broken, hurting little sister.

If I were completely honest, the last month has really made me question what I am doing, especially now that there is no end in sight with no actual court date set. It could be another couple of weeks, or it could be six more months. Thankfully, I am leaving soon to take Ashley to the airport. She is spending a week at some dance training event in New York City, the lucky dog! The closest airport is two hours away and, since Josh will be home keeping their daughter, I volunteered for the job of driving her. I am so looking forward to it, though, because I REALLY need to talk to her right now. I always really need to talk to her, even though I know what she is going to say every time. I pull up to her house, help her throw her things in my small trunk, and off we go. But before I can begin to spill out my self-pity and loneliness, she begins.

"You would not believe the dreams I have had about you the past couple of nights," she says. The Lord frequently gives her dreams and, unfortunately for me, they are usually right on—and nothing that I want to hear. Fortunately for me she doesn't seem to want to share them. Instead there comes something worse, when all I wanted was to hang out with my friend for a couple of hours.

"Do you mind if I just pray over you while you drive?" she asks.

"Go right ahead," I reply doing a poor job at hiding my sarcasm and frustration.

She proceeds to pray, but not for freedom for me. Instead she prays for the marriage to be restored, for my heart to be turned back to Casey, for every voice that would speak against my marriage to be stopped. She prays and prophesies over Casey, myself, and the girls for the entire two-hour drive to the airport. As she steps out of the car she turns back to me, "I am still believing for you guys, Linds. And I will keep believing."

I just nod without looking at her as she closes the door.

For the two-hour drive back I contemplate her dream and all she prayed for. What if she is right? The more I think about it, the more I come to the conclusion that although I don't want the marriage, maybe I should at least give it a go. At least to be able to say I tried once. I decide I am going to go for it. It won't work out, but maybe, no, hopefully it will shut everyone up.

As soon as I get home that afternoon I call my attorney to have her put the divorce on hold. "Please DO NOT cancel it," I tell her. "Just put it on standby or something. I have to try to see if it can possibly work, if for no other reason than so I can at least go to sleep with a clear conscience. Would something like that be possible?"

"Well, not necessarily," Dianne answers. "As soon as a divorce is filed it is pretty much in motion until the judge signs it or until both parties agree to completely end it, and that is a whole separate process all to itself."

Well, this is just great. I can't even put my divorce on hold to even try to repair things. I don't want to completely stop it, I just want to stall things a bit, give me time to think things over and still be able to keep control of it all.

Dianne continues: "What you do have in your favor is that there isn't a set court date. I know we were hoping it would be soon but to be honest, Lindsey, I don't see that happening."

"Ok. Thank you," I reply.

"No problem. Call if you need anything else."

I decide to take her advice and at least use this waiting period as a time to try to fix it. Problem is, what if I decide that I want to fix it? What if I go all in and end up falling for him again? Then all my hard work really is over. Nonetheless, I have to give it a shot. I have to be able to say I tried. I am not going to tell Casey what I am doing— he will get his hopes up too much. This is something I have to do between God and me. Only God can change my heart anyway.

Thankfully it is Sunday and I don't have to go into work today or tomorrow, and Casey has the girls, so it gives me plenty of time to pray and find out what I want. I lay a blanket down on my floor, take my Bible and kneel down.

"God, you know my heart in this. You know that I really want out of the marriage. I ask you right now to release me from it so I will be at peace."

I wait . . . but I hear nothing.

"Please, Lord, tell me what You want me to do and where You want me to go. Please set me free from this place and these people. I want to minister to others but You know I cannot do it here."

Still nothing.

"Lord, change Casey. Change his heart. I know he is not the man You or I want him to be. Let him see truth, and break deception off of him and Mom both. God, if You change him then I might have a chance to be with him."

I go on for hours. I stop to eat dinner then go back to my blanket. I wait. God's Word says if I ask anything according to His will it shall be done, and that's exactly what I am doing. This is God's will isn't it? After another hour of silence I give up. I will try again tomorrow, but for now I am done asking God what to do and hearing nothing. This is more effort than I have put out in months, though, and for that I feel pretty good about myself and my decision to maybe fight for Casey and me. I cover up in the blanket I was using as my prayer mat, lie on my couch and turn on my TV. Nothing of any interest is on so I decide to spend some time on my new "Lindsey Reneé" Facebook page before I go to bed.

I have a message. I wait for it to load and hope it is not another "Praying for you; God can restore it; go back to Casey" message. I almost drop my phone as soon as the profile picture comes up. It's from a man I have not heard from in ten years.

"Hey, Angel! It's been a long time! How are you?" It is from Owen, my old high school fling. Angel was the name he gave me when I was fourteen. I am shocked he still remembers it.

Without thinking I immediately respond back, knowing I shouldn't—but what harm can come from it? It's not like anything is going to happen. I'm just checking in on an old friend. And I am so lonely any attention is better than nothing.

"Oh my gosh, Owen! It has been such a long time! How are you?!"

"Well, I am doing pretty well for myself. I ended up getting the job I always wanted. Have a beautiful little girl. I am currently separated from my wife at the moment. We will be divorcing soon but all is well. We are still friends."

"I am so sorry," I reply. "I hate to hear about what you are going through. I am in a very similar situation. My marriage is ending as well."

"That's rough, and pretty ironic. Listen, I know it is none of my business, but if you ever need someone to talk to, I'm here for you."

Maybe this is God's answer for me. Not to be with Owen romantically maybe, but perhaps it's His answer to not stop the divorce, to continue going on with my life, to continue walking toward freedom and happiness because it really is out there. If it's not God's answer, at least I am not totally alone in the loneliness of a separation. I am just completely unaware of how the enemy uses these things to make you believe it is an answer to prayer. I'm also completely unaware of what is about to happen over the next year.

Chapter 16

AUGUST

How do you willingly walk straight into a situation when you know it is going to hurt you? Why? Why does that happen? I knew better. I knew it to the core, and I walked right in anyway.

The day I heard back from Owen was a great one, or so I thought. I was hoping, if nothing else, we could get closure on our relationship since it had ended so abruptly when we were teenagers. My heart was shattered then. We had a very sinful and sexual relationship in high school and even after how far we'd gone together, he still broke my heart. Our relationship became baggage I took into my young marriage. I should have known better. Nothing happened over the few months we talked. He lived across the country so we never saw each other in person, but my heart did get involved since we talked so much. You'd think I would have learned by now how these friendships "just happen" to turn emotional. But I don't. It's the same mistake I continue to make over and over and over again.

Just as I had gotten used to having someone to talk to, he's gone. For a few months I wasn't alone. He gave me pity and friendship. Then, just like that. Nothing. How does it keep happening this way? Now it was almost Christmas. The last I heard from him, he sent one simple message, "I'm sorry. I can't do this anymore," and that was it. No explanation whatsoever. Now the only messages between me and Casey are hostile ones—well, at least mine are hostile. He still tries to present this "I am still being sweet to you despite your hatred toward me" front, but even after almost a year, I know more than ever that is all it is: a front. I am stunned he hasn't moved on already—it's not like he doesn't have a line of women waiting to throw themselves at his feet. I am chalking it up to the fact that if he did move on it would ruin his reputation.

As for me, I stopped caring about trying to keep my good reputation long ago. Filing for a divorce and all the blame that is thrown on you for it will do that to you. When you have nothing else to lose you really don't care what happens anymore, so I really don't understand why I feel the need to hide these friendships and relationships I'm having with other guys from Mom and Casey. There is no point in holding on to a marriage that is long lost. Dianne has assured me that nothing can be done against me legally as it pertains to the divorce as long as there isn't a man living in the house with me or hurting the girls. Heaven knows I would not go so far as to let that happen. So why do I still care? I am guessing it has to do with my desperate need to still have their approval in my life. Though I will never admit it. I miss them.

The gaping hole in me is growing more and more with each casualty this divorce causes. I am starting to lose count of the people I have lost—even people who started out on my side in this whole thing. Many of them have, as they say, "seen the truth in everything," and decided to cut me off. Others are just tired of my constant nagging and self-pity.

Some days are far easier than others. Some days I am strong and empowered and can take on anything that is thrown at me. Others are not so easy. Today is one of the tougher ones. The girls have their three-and-a-half days with Casey starting this afternoon after school, so tonight I will be completely alone, again. The constant spewing to people about Casey and Mom and the divorce and all that's been done to me is starting to run its course. Everyone I have been talking to has heard the story over and over again and really doesn't want to hear it anymore, but I am finding it is all I want to talk about. I can't get enough pity. I need more every day and people's supply of it for me is running low. All the friends I have gone to and lied to about Casey, saying he was abusive, just don't care much anymore. After all, I am out of the marriage now—well, technically speaking at least—so why keep complaining and talking about it? Maybe I just need to hear myself say it, to continue to convince myself that what I am doing is okay. Despite the continuation of days when I have no one there to talk to, and the near-constant pain and conflict inside me, life has started to flow into somewhat of a normal routine. Get up, get ready, drive the girls to Mom's, drive to work, come home. Not at all the life I expected or planned to have.

As I walk into work today I am greeted by August, a guy who usually works in the shipping department of the mall. It looks like today he is out on the floor doing some maintenance work.

"Hey! Lindsaaaay!" he says. I am *so* not in the mood for this today. I ignore him and go on to my station in the salon. He follows me in there. "Woah, what's going on?" he says, a bit more sincerely. "You're usually so . . . happy."

I shoot him a sarcastic look.

"Well, kind of."

I continue to set up my station for my first client. I am so deeply angry at myself for what I've done, getting emotionally involved with Owen, on top of everything happening between me and Mom, on top of everything happening between me and Casey! Can I not just move on and have a happy ending? I need to have someone in my life. Being alone is NOT what I expected it to be and I can't stand the pain of the loneliness any more. Regardless of the fact that I barely know August, other than his name and that he works in the warehouse, I finally erupt on him.

"It's just . . . everything, August! It's the fact that I filed for a divorce and I don't know if that is the right decision, not at all. I have no end in sight for it to be over,

I am working at a salon in a mall after having to walk away from everything I have ever known, and this is not even close to what I want to do. I've lost my family, all my friends, I have no one in my life! I have no money here, and I will probably never be able to get full custody of my girls and be able to leave this place. I still love everyone at home, and hate them so much at the same time! I desperately want to be left alone, but still need their stamp of approval every waking minute! I feel like I'm dying! I am losing everything! It is all slipping through my hands like sand and I can control none of it! I have nobody! None! Just leave me alone, August."

"Well, I'm here. You have me," he says.

I roll my eyes. "I don't even know you. You're just another guy working here at the mall."

"Wow, so polite, too!" he says.

"Just leave me alone. Please. I'll be in a better mood later." I hear his name being called over the intercom. Thank God.

"Listen," he continues, "why don't you come by my place tonight? You can vent all you want. It will be just me and my roommate there." I don't reply. He quickly writes down his number, leaves it on my station and walks out.

A fellow employee walks over to where I stand. "I think he may have a thing for you, Lindsey."

"Yeah, well, tough luck," I reply. I am in no mood to hear about men and whether or not they are interested in me.

My shift ends several hours later. My mood did lighten up, and August came by to talk to me anytime he was in close vicinity. It was a slow day for the salon, for which I am thankful. I couldn't handle the constant gossip and chatter of clients all day—not today, anyway. I finally get to pack up my station and leave. It is my turn to close the salon down so I will have to stay a little longer than I normally would. Most of the employees are gone by the time I make it out.

August is standing at the door when I go to the computer to clock out. "Hey, thought I would wait on you. Any chance you wanna take me up on coming by tonight? No pressure though. Just thought you might need a friend." I know he will never leave me alone so I decide to go.

"Why not," I reply. I have nothing to do tonight anyway and if nothing else I can kill some time before I have to head home to my dark and lonely hole on the hill.

"Great!" he says as he opens the door to leave. "It's just a couple of miles from here. You can follow me." The minute I close the door to my car I feel the most intense warnings of danger.

Run, Lindsey. Run now.

What is the big deal? I am going to hang out with a guy from work. We are not even friends. It's not like anything is going to happen.

DO NOT DO THIS.

There are no other cars in his driveway as I pull in. There's no one there but me and him. Odd. "Hey, I thought your roommates were going to be here?" I say.

"Oh, they were. They had to leave for work a few minutes ago, got called onto a different shift. It's okay if we still hang out though, right?"

"Well, yeah, it's fine, but I have a long drive back so I can't stay long." A smile spreads across his face as he walks me to his door. I hear it close behind me and know this will be no short visit.

When I walk back out of his house alone, I know I have crossed a line that I will never be able to uncross for the rest of my life. Some traps catch you by surprise. Some you walk into with eyes wide open. I have sunk to a new low I never thought I would experience. I have become the harlot. Never, in my wildest dreams, did I ever think I would go so low as to have a one-night stand. But anyone is capable of anything—and here I am. How can I ever look into Casey's face again? As much as I want to excuse my actions, I can't. I know it's not a big deal in the world's eyes but this is a huge deal to me. I have become exactly what I was as a teenage girl. I turned right back into the person Casey helped change and heal. Now I have cheated on him, in every way that one can. I have given my heart to some, my mind to others, and now my body.

Dear God, what have I become?

Any shot I would have had at making the marriage work is truly gone now. There is no recovering from this. I have thrown away my last chance. What will happen in the divorce if anyone finds out? Suddenly, paranoia fills me. I could lose my girls. Can I lose them for this? They weren't here, but still, can I have them taken from me for sleeping with someone? Heaven knows, they don't deserve a mother like me. They deserve so much better. So much more than what I am. But I will never give them up. I cannot lose them. What will my mother think? And my sister? What will Casey think? They can never know. Never. I will never, ever find myself in this place again.

I block August's number from my phone. I block him on every form of social media I can think of, even though we are friends on none of them. I am so disgusted with myself I don't know what to do. The only place lower than this point would be death, and even that may actually be a step up for me.

That morning I quit my job. My boss asks the reason since, after a couple of months, I had finally started to do pretty well there. Of course I can't give the real one. What am I supposed to say? "Oh, I stooped so low as to sleep with a guy here at work and I can't stand myself or my life so I quit"? Instead, I come up with an excuse about the drive being too hard and how I have opportunities back at home—but there are no opportunities at home. The shame I have is unbearable. I thought I was numb to guilt, numb to my reputation, but now I am feeling things I have never felt before. I have never felt so low, so filthy. I am the whore. I deserve no mercy, no pity, not from anyone. I do not dare ask God for forgiveness. I can never be forgiven of this. I will never be able to forgive myself, and I will never try.

Chapter 17

THAT STILL SMALL VOICE

If you have children you'll know how difficult it can be to get their attention at times, especially as they grow older and develop a mind and will of their own. Our oldest daughter Analeise has a deep passion for music. When she has her headphones on she cannot hear me talking to her. It is not that my voice is absent, it is that something else is taking her attention by filling her ears and mind. In order to hear me she has to remove what is distracting her attention. When she does, she is able to hear me clearly. In the same way, God's voice is there for us. It is within us. When we are filled with the Holy Spirit, it is that peace we feel, the whisper we hear in the moments we are alone and quiet. His voice is there to warn us, correct us, guide us, teach us, forgive and change us. But we have to take the headphones off.

In the middle of my situation I found myself trying to drown out His voice more and more. I distracted myself with countless hours of music and movies. If not that, I would make sure I was always on the phone talking to someone, filling my thoughts with their voice and advice. As soon as I'd hang up the phone I'd call another person. And another. And another. I allowed other people to take the place of the Holy Spirit. I allowed others to guide me in what I should do. Still, in the midst of all the distractions, He would speak, but I was the one who would not listen. Not only did I not listen, I would take His words and twist them. But still He spoke. He spoke through others, through dreams, through His written Word, through warnings—and I ignored it all for two years. The more I ignored, the more clogged my ears became.

When that voice becomes quieter and quieter, it is not that the Lord has stopped speaking. It is because we have stopped hearing. We have stopped listening. What a frightening moment it is to be disconnected from His voice! When we choose to drown His voice out, it is then we are given over to our own tormenting thoughts.

There is a quote by Blaise Pascal that states, "All of humanity's problems stem from man's inability to sit quietly in a room alone.[2]" Of course, that is not the reason for *all* of humanity's problems; however, look at the meaning behind the statement. Have you ever tried

2   *Pensées*, Blaise Pascal, 1669

sitting quietly in a room alone, even for just an hour? No phone, no music, no TV, nothing. No distractions at all. Your thoughts begin to run wild. You relive so much that has been tormenting your thoughts. When we are not walking closely with the Lord, when we are walking outside of His will, those dark thoughts consume us. Why? Because we have distracted ourselves with what WE want or what others have to say about our situations. I want to challenge you to try this experiment: go somewhere where you can be completely alone and sit for an hour, no distractions at all. Just sit. After the hour goes by, take a journal and write down the thoughts that come to mind. How freeing would it be to finally be able to sit alone and be at complete peace? No shame, no torment, no dark thoughts at all. Not only to be at peace, but to be able to hear those sweet whispers of the Holy Spirit again. It would be the most beautiful sound in the world.

Even during our hardest times, He is there, always speaking; but it is in the hard times we must listen with caution, as it is so easy to misunderstand or, even worse, listen through the filter of deception. Remember, what God speaks will only confirm what is in His Word. He will not contradict Himself, and He will not allow His voice to be manipulated and twisted so we can get our own way.

John 10:27 (AMP) says this, "The sheep that are My own hear My voice and listen to Me; I know them, and they follow Me." There is no mistaking the voice of God.

When He speaks, there is no question as to what He is saying. God does not torment us with riddles that must be figured out. He doesn't come with confusion. He knows everything we need. He knows exactly what to say to help us grow and change and walk in peace, joy, and rest.

There are roughly 7.5 billion people on earth. There are 196 countries and approximately 6,500 spoken languages. But God doesn't speak 6,500 languages—He speaks 7.5 billion. God speaks YOUR language. He speaks MY language. The Lord knows every method possible of reaching every person on earth. He knows what catches your attention. He knows how to reach you in the best and in the very worst of times. Because of this, the only way we cannot hear what He has to say is if we willingly ignore, or alter, what He says. That prick you feel when you are about to do something against His will, that is Him. That peace that fills you when you choose to walk down the road He is guiding you on, Him again. But it is up to us to act upon that voice. Should we choose wrong, it is the consequence of that choice that will be the punishment. Should we choose to obey His leading, it is peace that will follow.

If you find that you can't hear Him, try taking off your own headphones, the things in your life that are distracting you, and see what He has to say about your situation. Do not try to listen with your own intentions in mind. Listen with no motive other than what HE wants for you. The voice of the Lord is always there, though at times it can seem He has stopped talking and left us, especially when we are living in a sinful lifestyle and we no longer listen to Him. It is due to the lies we have created for ourselves—our shame, our condemnation, our lifestyle, the voices of others—that can most often drown out that still small voice. So, go ahead and shut everything and everyone out. What is He saying to you? Can you hear Him now?

Chapter 18

OWNERSHIP

There is no greater agony than bearing an untold story
inside you. [3]
Maya Angelou

They say there are always two sides to any story, two sides to every court case or lawsuit, two sides to every broken marriage. I disagree. There is only one side—and that is your side.

Now, before you misunderstand me, let me explain what I mean. "There is only your side" does not mean your side the right side, nor does it make your side the wrong one. It simply means you are responsible ONLY for your side of a story. That means every decision, action, choice, word, hidden thought, and secret desire, as well as the consequences of those things, are the fault of only one person: you.

---

[3]   *I Know Why the Caged Bird Sings* (Virago, 1984)

2 Corinthians 5:10 (The Message) states, "Sooner or later we'll all have to face God, regardless of our conditions. We will appear before Christ and take what's coming to us as a result of *our* actions, either good or bad" (emphasis mine.) When we stand before God, at the end of all things, we will give an account for OUR side of the story, not the deeds or actions of someone else or, better yet, someone we say has wronged us. Excuses like, "I did this because he said that to me", or, "I said that to her because my feelings were hurt", may work when talking to friends and family who want to keep us victimized in someone else's side of the story, but it will not work when we are standing before the eyes of Christ. On that day, there will be no room for blame-casting, defenses, or excuses. On that day, we will be asked, "What did YOU do? Give YOUR account." That is what I mean when I say your side is the only side. It is the only side you have. It is the only side of a story you are allowed to tell. It means growing up, owning up, and taking responsibility for our lives.

What does it mean, exactly, to take responsibility for our side of a story? If we were completely honest, for many of us, coming clean has a trail of consequences behind it. Sometimes living with the past and all we have done wrong is WAY easier than facing our past and the people in it. It is so much easier to just shove it all down and escape than to feel the pain of it all over again. Coming clean and taking responsibility for our actions means we have to face the past again, even after we've been running from it for years, or even decades. Facing it means we will have to feel it all over again. We not only have to face our actions, we also have to face the consequences of those actions, and the people we hurt. This is one of the roots of shame—the fear of facing what has once been done; not only the action itself, but the fear of facing the pain of it again.

Some of those painful past memories are from things done to us, but many are from things we have done to others; memories of shameful events or actions that have cost us so much. For some, it costs their purity as teenagers, or perhaps it costs their purity as children. For others, it is the pain of knowing it was they who took another child's purity, it was they who put the drug in the girl's drink and took her home that dark night. It was they who decided to open their heart to someone other than their husband or wife. It was they who neglected their own children for a job. It was they who drove home drunk and cost the life of another. It was they who offered the needle to a friend, only to see that friend collapse and never breathe again. It was they who secretly looked at pictures of naked men or women when everyone else was asleep. Maybe it is the girl who holds the positive pregnancy test, thinking, "My mother is going to kill me," while the unborn child is thinking the exact same thing. Maybe it is the woman who wakes up from the nightmares of hearing the sound of the vacuum that ripped the baby out of her womb. Maybe it is the pastor who secretly desires his female, or even male, assistant. Maybe it is the stay-at-home mom who secretly texts, emails, and messages her old high school boyfriend while her husband is at work. Maybe it is the youth pastor sending inappropriate pictures of himself to a young teenage boy in his youth group. Maybe it is the person reading this book who was able to immediately place themselves in one or more of these examples. The list can go on forever.

Secrets and lies, lies and secrets. Hiding the phone calls and messages from that secret "friendship" that is not really a relationship yet but is well on its way and already completely inappropriate; or burying the memories of the face and screams of that little child who let out a paralyzed plea as their purity was ripped from them. Never telling a soul, never speaking of it again but, deep down, living with the shame and regret of it all. You already know God knows, but that is not really where the fear comes from. You can't be afraid to tell something to someone who already knows it. It is the fear of telling it to ourselves again, confessing and hearing the words come out of our mouths that we actually did it. The pain of that is unbearable. The memory is unbearable. To hear the words, and relive it all over again—this is difficult for anyone and no one is exempt from the pain of it. But let's take it a step further than just reliving it ourselves. Think about the things that are, right now, being hidden from the people in your life, things that are being hidden from your husband, your wife, your parents, friends, or family. Now ask yourself this question: What would these people do if they, too, knew?

There are countless reasons why each person hides the shameful memories of their lives. I have found three to be the most prominent. The first is the shallowest and most obvious reason to hide anything: because of the sheer embarrassment you would feel if what you were hiding were exposed. But the deception of embarrassment is that it is so easy to confuse it with shame. For example, embarrassment says, "If I tell someone what I have done, I will forever be embarrassed by what they know and it will be held over my head forever. If people know, I will never get away from it." However, shame works by staying in your head. It holds you captive by the memories and the thoughts that you think about yourself. It's the voice in the back of your head that rebuts everything good that you try to say or do with "But remember why you are not qualified . . ."

The second reason we hide is that we don't want to hurt people we love. We ask ourselves the question, "What would my wife do if she found out?" We say things like, "It would crush my children. My parents wouldn't be able to look at me." Yes, those are all valid issues. Sometimes we think that lying and hiding are simply the right decisions to make. It would save those that we love from suffering. The problem with that is, in the midst of all of those questions, have we included God's opinion? Anytime we lie we keep God from that area of our life. We have it protected from Him by our own words. Do we not trust that if we give Him the entirety of our lives, that He can even bring good from the bad? Lying protects the "old" version of ourselves. Lying is making an agreement with that old version. What could be more hurtful to those you love than that? When we protect our sin, protect our "wrongness," we give shame the right to thrive.

Lastly, hiding helps us protect the life we are living. Ultimately, hiding protects the decisions that we know are wrong but still want to make. However, if people found out our secrets and lies, that would be the end of it. There would no longer be the option to go back to the lie. If exposed, it would then become inconvenient to continue living in the sin and the lie that we have found comfort in. Sometimes people lie and hide for this simple reason: they do not want to change.

Would you believe me if I told you it is absolutely possible to live your life completely in the open, with everyone knowing everything, and there not be an ounce of embarrassment, fear, or dread in you of what people know? Would you believe me if I told you it is possible to be completely forgiven and to live utterly free of everything, NO MATTER HOW BAD IT IS? Some of you might think, "Well, you don't know what I've done, how deep my story goes." My answer to that is, you don't really know how deep the love of God goes. He already knows what you have done. He already saw it when it happened.

He didn't strike you dead after it happened, He didn't gasp in shock. In fact, He knew it was going to happen before it happened. So what is there to hide? You are only hiding from yourself and others at this point, but not from God. You can't hide from God. If you're reading this then you are still breathing, and if you're still breathing then He is waiting on you to take the first step to freedom. Realizing you may be bound to the shame of your past or current actions is the first step to freedom.

So what happens when you decide to own up to everything: the good, the bad and the ugly? What happens when you drag all the skeletons out of the closet and say, "Here it is! I am responsible for all this. I did all of this. I am hiding all of this pain"? What happens when you truly repent? What happens when you get so desperate for freedom and truth that you are willing to do whatever it takes—you'll cut off friendships or relationships, throw away anything? What happens? Judgment? Condemnation? Guilt? Rejection? That is certainly what I expected to receive for my own past action—and heaven knows, I would have deserved it. Instead I found this: defeated shame. But how?

Chapter 19

DEFEATED SHAME

Have you ever stood before a judge in a courtroom knowing you are at the absolute mercy of whatever he or she decides? Have you ever stood before a judge knowing that, regardless of the lies you have told everyone else, every accusation against you is correct—and just to make things worse, that judge already knows about all of it and saw it all happen? You stand there, head downcast, knowing there is absolutely no way you're gonna be able to lie, defend or talk your way out of this one. You look up and see the judge reading the case against you, and you wait. You wait for the gavel to come down, accompanied by the words "guilty as charged". You begin to imagine what your life will be like once you hear the echo of those words. A dark life, a cursed life. Every person you have ever known looking at you and whispering to another, "Did you hear about her story?" Always wearing the scarlet letter of sin and shame. You know, with every fiber of your being, that you deserve whatever punishment the judge passes down; and strangely, in the midst of all the dread and fear, there is an odd peace in you, because you know on that case written against you, you've finally said it all. You told your story. You faced it again, you owned up to what you did with no defenses or excuses.

You glance over at the accuser's table and see his sly smile. Relaxing in his chair, he, too, saw what happened; he, too, waits for the pronouncement of judgment. You know this time he has won—after all you've done, how could he not win? All the evidence is stacked up against you. Closing your eyes you finally hear the strike of the gavel. It echoes across the silent room, then comes the judge's voice.

"Clear the accused of all charges."

Just like that it's over. It's done. The accuser, shrieking and writhing, is taken from the room. You can't even rejoice, out of the sheer shock of what has just happened. You KNOW you are guilty. You KNOW you deserve the fullness of the punishment. You yourself owned up to and admitted all of your wrongdoing! But instead of judgment you hear "cleared of all charges." There has to be a mistake. As you look back up, you see no judge; instead, you see a Father, with grace in His eyes and mercy in His extended hands. Perfect love. Unconditional love. Absolute forgiveness. Complete freedom.

Matthew 10:28 (The Message) says, "Don't be bluffed into silence by the threat of bullies. There's nothing they can do to your soul, your core being. Save your fear for

God, who holds your entire life—body and soul—in His hands."

There are many things that begin the path to shame, and many things that keep us there, but for those who want out, the first step to destroying shame is to go before God, taking all of your story to Him—no defenses, no excuses for any of your actions, no blaming someone else for anything that you've done, no victimizing yourself, no hiding anything—and, in the place of judgment, receiving mercy, love, and grace. When that happens, every previous fear you had of how people will look at you if you told your story, what people would say if they knew what really happened, is gone. All the fear is gone. How? Why? Because you looked in the face of a just God—a God that holds the fate of both body and soul in His hands—and received grace. Nothing else will ever measure up to a moment like that. No other opinion even comes close. Then, when people do whisper and gossip and slander (and believe me they will), all you hear is, "Cleared of all charges." In that moment, the whispers don't matter.

When people from your past come back around and remind you of who you were and the things you did, you feel no shame. Regardless of their reaction, you hear, "Go in freedom." And then, in that moment, those people don't matter. You are forgiven. You are absolutely and completely forgiven; a blank slate, a new story, life starting completely over. If you read that and, in the back of your mind, still feel a twinge of pain, a desire to hide from something in your past, or if a moment of wrongdoing comes back into thought, there may still be shame. When you know you are forgiven, it's not that you don't remember what happened—you do remember what happened but the only One who could hold it against you chooses not to. Your past will always call back to you; there will always be things that trigger memories. But there doesn't always have to be shame.

Shame is something every person on the planet has or will have to deal with at some point in their lives. It is impossible for anybody to live the entirety of their life and never experience it. However, for some of us, shame can become more than a moment in time; it can become a life-long prison for our minds. Shame is the lie we believe about ourselves. It can be cast upon us through experiences or it can be lived out through our own decisions and choices. Most often, however, those two things work hand-in-hand.

For example, let's look at this little girl's story.

Gracie lives in a beautiful home with her parents and two sisters. Although she loves her family very much, and they love her, she is constantly hearing statements from her parents like, "You're so stupid, Gracie, why can't you be more like your sister? You are a very bad little girl. When are you going to grow up? You're never going to amount to anything." As she grows, Gracie begins to live up to the identity she was given as a child. Thus, the cycle of shame begins. Because she has grown up believing she is stupid, bad, childish, and worth nothing, she goes into her teenage life making decisions based on those beliefs. She truly believes she is stupid so she slacks on her schoolwork. She believes she is, in her nature, bad so she behaves badly. She believes she is immature so she acts out. She believes she is worth nothing, so she hooks up with guys who give her the false sense of security she is craving, but leave her just as empty and worthless as before. Her actions as a teenage girl leave her in regret as an adult. She eventually marries and carries all the shame and baggage of her childhood and youth into her marriage and job. Now, as an adult, Gracie continues her lifestyle of poor decisions, wrong friends, and sinful relationships. She eventually ends up divorced, her kids split between homes, struggling to put food on the table for herself and her family. Instead of recognizing what is really happening, she decides to put the responsibility of her actions and choices on her parents, the friends she grew up with, and her ex-husband. Why? Because shame never exposes itself. It hides behind others through blame-casting, excuses, and defenses. Shame tells her what she is (stupid, bad, childish, etc.), but blames others for those beliefs and her actions. She swears to herself she will not do the same thing to her children but, sadly, if her beliefs and lifestyle go undealt with, her children will suffer the same fate she did.

Gracie's story is an example of how shame can begin

by being cast upon us, and also how it continues in us, growing and imprisoning us through our own beliefs, choices, actions, and regrets as adults. We all have our own stories of shame, bondage, and regrets. Some stories are severe, some not so much; some just moments of embarrassment or guilt, and others tormenting lifelong mental prison sentences. But it is never God's will for us to continue to live in shame or torment. It is His will for us to live a glorious and free life. That life is available to all. We need only to reach out to our forgiving Father and take it.

Chapter 20

PICKING UP THE PIECES

The sun is setting on a beautiful Fall afternoon. I have a lovely tree standing right outside my salon in Hamilton that continues to amaze me with its daily transformation of color. Why can't our own transformations be so effortless? In the last month I have tried desperately to transform myself. My hair is now an ultra short, half-shaved pixie cut. I've lost a few pounds, and have completely changed my wardrobe: shorter bottoms, lower tops, and lots and lots of black. It's my not-so-great attempt at trying to remake myself in some form or fashion. Although I am finally my own woman, everything about me doesn't quite feel like me. I am certain that, over time, those feelings will change, though.

I am waiting (not so patiently) for my last client of the day to arrive. Thank goodness she is just a cut and style. If I can get out of here soon enough I am taking the girls to Tupelo for dinner. It is always a good (and safe) getaway when my thoughts begin to torment me which, after my incident with August, is all the time now. Even after all this time I will not forgive myself for what I did with him. Never. I never will, and neither will God, neither will Casey. I cannot get clean of it. I could scrub myself until even my skin peeled off and I would not be clean. The filth is coming from within, seeping through every part of me. I have destroyed Casey, I have destroyed myself, I have destroyed my children. I force myself to feel nothing now. To feel anything would end me. I have become utterly numb, like a tower of granite, impenetrable to pain, to guilt, to anything or anyone. I feel nothing. I refuse to. If this is what this life I chose looks like, it is not what I wanted at all. No one knows, and no one will ever know. Not even Daddy, and he's the only person I can trust.

Daddy keeps telling me things will get better. He and the fragile few friends I have left are furious there is still no finality to the divorce. Now, because of the circumstances surrounding the name of our ministry and our family's reputation, our divorce has been through three judges until finally being sent to the Alabama Supreme Court for them to assign a judge to handle it, one who doesn't know Mother or the ministry. The perk to that? No one will be able to show favoritism to Casey because of what he is connected to. Also, neither Mom nor anyone in the ministry could try to contact and sway the judge in any direction. Could they actually do that? Probably not, but at this point I do believe they would try if they got desperate enough. And are they ever desperate!

The "words" people continue to give me about God wanting to save me and my marriage are endless. At this point, I don't even care anymore. They can get over it. I have stopped answering the phone calls and messages of pastors who used to be in my life. They remind me of the conviction and standard I used to live by and it makes me feel things I refuse to ever feel again. I have finally determined to live by my own convictions. If I feel like drinking, I will drink. If I want to go out with friends, I will go. If I want to be in a relationship, I will be in it. I will not ever let them get to me again. I will not let anyone get to me. I rarely speak to my biological mother or sister now. My stepmother, Joyce, and her children have replaced my mother and sister. Anyone who chooses my ex over me is no family of mine. My girls are welcome to have a relationship with my family, but I never will again. At least, not like it used to be. I don't want it, and if they were really honest—which they're not—neither do they. So they can get what they asked and wished for: a life without Lindsey. Sure, I will show up to holidays and such, but only for the sake of the girls. Nothing more.

In the past year I have found myself in two more relationships, but I have now learned how to do them right. I've learned to only get involved to a certain point so I will never hurt myself or regret anything ever again. The first guy, Jayden, came into my life not long after

August went out. He was someone to talk to, but I refused to let him get too close. Like Owen he, too, lived on the other side of the country but actually came down a couple of times to meet up. Nothing sexual happened this time, other than the couple of times he kissed me before he left to head back home. He also brought some of his own family to visit so everything stayed safe. I am never going to put myself into a situation where I could end up making the same mistake I did with August. The guy I am currently talking to—Logan—is more of a "best friend" than anything. He fills the loneliness gap when no one else is around to do so. However, I fear that he is diving in emotionally far more than I am. But I don't control him, and as long as I am not the one that gets hurt, I really don't care.

I finally decided to get over the fear of what Mom or Casey would try to do and have allowed the girls around my string of guys more frequently. Although I am long from having any kind of serious relationship, the girls need to get used seeing someone else around. I know I will never replace Casey as their father, and I can honestly say I don't even want to, regardless of what happens between me and him. I DO NOT want them to lose their relationship with their dad as children in the same way I did. Even today, though my relationship with my father Scott is better than it has ever been, it is still splintered from the nearly two decades of a bad one, and I don't want my girls to experience that. Casey is a great father—I can lie about a lot but that remains true. He loves his two girls more than anything.

However much I try to make it not a big deal, the girls can't stand other men. I keep trying to reassure them that life will be happy, no matter who is around, and NO ONE will ever replace them. No one will, ever. That is also a fact. They really are the most important people in the world to me. The day I can finally escape where we live and the three of us can start completely over, and I can hopefully pursue that long-lost dance company dream, will truly be the best day of my life. I will be able to get them out. I'll be able to open up that company somewhere in Florida, near Daddy. I will finally be free. Until then I have had to make some choices that will keep me here for just a little while longer. But that is a sacrifice I am willing to make as long as the girls and I can end up free in the long run.

Needing a source of solid income I have opened my own salon in Hamilton and am doing pretty well for myself. It is by no means where I want to be working but it is far easier on the girls. I don't have extra money, by any means, and I still need extra financial support every once in a while, but I can put food on the table and cover most of my bills at least. I've had to ask Mom for money sometimes, which is humiliating, and she's had to bail me out of some pretty tough situations. I do appreciate her help and she seems pretty sincere in her generosity, but I still can't shake that nagging feeling that she may be doing it just to be able to prove to other people that she is trying to make some sort of effort of kindness toward me. It's just another show, just another way to make her look good, or so I choose to believe .

Although no one in my family knows, I have rented an apartment and will soon move from Hamilton to Florence. It's not anywhere close to where I want to be, but Florence will be good for me. I have no problem with my family knowing about me moving, I just really don't want to hear the comments and see the faces and know, as soon as I walk out of the door, they will be there talking about "How I am making such bad decisions for my life." I've never known a family to gossip about each other the way mine does.

The commute to work and home will be terrible again. Instead of living in Hamilton and working in Florence, now I will be living in Florence and working in Hamilton. It won't be forever, though. I will be able to get completely away soon enough, even if it's not as soon as I thought. If nothing else, at least I will be able to control who the girls are around when they are with me, and I won't have anyone breathing down my neck trying to see who is at the house with me and them.

The girls will be happy living in Florence, I know it. Heaven knows, they need to get away from the family toxicity. A couple of friends of mine connected me up with a church there. We have been attending the last several months and, to be honest, it's pretty amazing. The pastors are, of course, completely for the restoration of my marriage, but they try to stay out of the details of it, for the most part. A few people from Mom's ministry attend that church as well. Needless to say, I avoid them as much as humanly possible. I know I shouldn't care if they try to go and tattle on my every move, but even then, I don't want to involve myself in any way with anyone associated with that awful place. It is so nice to finally have somewhere to go. There was no church in Hamilton I could safely attend without being followed around or ratted out, so I had been doing my own devotions at home by myself on the Sundays I was alone, and I'd do them in Tupelo for those days out when I had the girls. The people at this church are great people. Talented people. I even have some dance opportunities there for the time being. It is not my dream for a dance company and school by any means, but it does give me an outlet to do something with dancing.

Eighteen months since I filed. Eighteen months! I am trying to keep it out of court and finally have a mediation date scheduled for next month. I have spent the last year getting as much evidence together as I can to try and get as much custody of the girls as possible. Yeah, Casey is a great dad, but I want to get them more, and I want to drive the knife into him as far as I can. There is one last thing for me to do before I face him again: a week at an inner healing retreat with Ashley at Restoring the Foundations. Her husband Josh was beyond generous to gift me with the week-long trip with her. I've not looked forward to something so much in a long, long time. Besides getting to hang with my best friend for that long and it being just us girls, I am hoping it will give me some closure within myself and give me some much-needed peace before I walk into my final mediation. After the Restoring the Foundations retreat I can finally start to close this chapter of my life.

My client's car finally pulls up. I quickly go ahead and set up my supplies so as to save as much time as possible. I am ready to get out of this town for the evening. I am ready to spend the next week with Ashley. I am ready to FINALLY close this chapter and move on with my life.

Chapter 21

RESTORING THE FOUNDATIONS

"How can we pray for you, Lindsey? Today we are dealing with word curses, but before we start we want to be able to pray with and for you and get a take on where you are after the first couple of sessions," say my remarkable Restoring the Foundations counselors. They have been with this ministry for years and are a charming older couple. Trustworthy. Loving. Sincere in their desire to help me. They've been married for years, and have faced and conquered many hardships together. They give me hope for a happy, healthy relationship for myself one day.

Thus far, this week could not have gone better. Ashley and I are staying only a couple of miles from the Restoring the Foundations location. The venue sits at the top of the beautiful Blue Ridge Mountains of North Carolina. The views are stunning and, more than anything, I am far away from everyone in Hamilton and getting to spend a glorious week with one of the only people I truly care about and genuinely trust. I can't be vulnerable with everyone, but I know I am safe with Ashley.

Our first session was more or less like an interview, a time for them to get an idea of where I am spiritually and emotionally. They just listened. Listened and prayed—something I have been desperately needing far more than I thought I did. So many people have given me advice. It was unusual for me to have someone just listen and really not care about anything other than seeing me healed and whole, regardless of who caused the damage inside of me—even if I was the one who did it to myself. Though I don't believe I need to be "healed or whole," I still appreciate their effort, attention, and care. More than they know.

The second session was a day to repent, to dig into past sins and faults of not only myself but of my family for generations back, and find where my mindsets, beliefs, and habits may have generated from. Today, however, is new territory for me. It is word curses. Heaven knows, it is going to be a long day for them. I can go on forever about how everyone has done me wrong and spoken terrible things about me.

"How can you pray for me?" I ask them back. "Well, do you want the short list or the long list?" They laugh and I allow them to just pray whatever it is they feel for that day. They begin to lead me into my session.

"Close your eyes, Lindsey. Allow the Lord to show you a moment that hurt you, a moment that something was spoken against you. Not something that hurt your feelings per se, but something that changed who you are, something that affected your identity."

I quickly write down several statements. I am expecting them to lead me into a long prayer about how the Lord will heal me and punish these people. Instead I am led into a prayer of forgiveness, releasing them from what they said and receiving what the Lord says about me instead. Next comes something I do not expect.

"Now, Lindsey, write down things you have said about others, curses you have placed on them." I immediately become defensive. What do they mean curses I have placed on others? I've done nothing wrong. How could they assume any of this is my fault?

"I've not cursed anyone," I reply.

"Well, have you ever accused your husband of anything you know to not be true? Anything you have said about your mother or your family? Anything you have gossiped or lied about? Have you ever attached a title to them that would label them as anything against the will of God?"

I look away knowing in my heart they are right. Admitting it is another thing entirely, though. There is silence for a long while in my small counseling room and I can feel them staring at me. I don't want to write anything, because nothing I have said is wrong. It's all true, at least in my mind it is. Ok, so none of the things I've said about my family and Casey is true at all. But it is how I have wanted it to be perceived, and that is all that matters anyway.

Just walk out, Lindsey. You don't deserve to be pushed into a corner this way.

I could walk out. I could skip this session. But if I do they will just pick it back up tomorrow. And besides, Ashley will ask me about it when it's over. They'll never leave me alone until I do it. What harm can come from writing a list of things I've said? It doesn't mean anything. It doesn't mean I have to think it was wrong. I'll just write down my own facts. . .

I called Casey an abuser

I labeled him as stupid

I labeled him a narcissist

I called Casey a liar

I said Casey would never change

I called him selfish

I called him a tyrant

I said he would never love me

I said he had no love in him for anyone

I said he would never amount to anything

I said he was a failure as a husband

The list goes on and on, countless things I accused him of, countless things I lied about to others. After I finish they lead me into another prayer, a prayer to release *him* from *my* words and curses and beliefs about him; a prayer to ask for forgiveness for speaking them over him and casting an identity on Casey that was not God's will for him.

As I look at my list, repenting for what I have said about him, I begin to question myself. Suddenly, after months of numbing myself, I am beginning to feel. I don't want to feel. I hate feeling. So small at first, but it is there. A question. Not like I think the answer would be "Yes", but still, I wonder. Was this me? No. It couldn't have been. I wasn't wrong; I was done wrong. I have to keep telling myself that. But the more I ponder, the more I begin to question. Was I really the one who did this, who caused the divorce? Was I the one who was wrong? Everything I have accused him of I actually did to him—and worse. I choose not to say anything to my counselors about this nagging question. It is probably nothing more than a fleeting emotion in the midst of a moment I have gotten caught up in. It will be gone by tomorrow.

That night Ashley and I head to downtown Asheville like we have each night after our sessions. We come down to eat dinner and wander around the town.

"Girl, my session today was so intense," she says to me. "There was so much in me I didn't even know was there! I think my eyes are still swollen from the crying. How did yours go?"

"Mine was amazing, too. No tears for me, but some things I didn't expect," I say.

"Uh huh," she says, cutting me a side-glance. I know what she is thinking and she is wrong. I don't miss Casey. I won't let myself miss him, no matter how much she wants me to. However, I still can't seem to get that horrible question out of my head: Was it me? I have spent so long believing he really didn't want me, that who I was wasn't enough. I had convinced myself that I could justify leaving the marriage because he was the one who didn't want to be together, but was just too much of a coward to say so. That evolved to the abuse allegations that evolved to him being a power hungry, dangerous narcissist. But what if I am wrong? What if those are all things I am in fact doing to him? What if I'm believing a lie—my own lie? I brush off the thought and change the subject. We spend the rest of the night talking about our kids and husbands. Well, ex-husband for me. I really wish she would stop asking me to tell her funny stories about Casey, or memories I have of when we were together. With what happened today in my session, her questions are starting to bring back happy times I have long forced myself to forget.

Three days later it is time to head home. Ashley and I say our goodbyes for now but I will see her again soon. I am about halfway into my eight-hour drive back to Hamilton and desperately need some music or conversation to fill the dead space. After leaving such a spiritual experience it doesn't seem right to turn on my usual secular playlist consisting of every "I hate my life and everyone in it" song I could find. And since I have no one I can call for conversation, I plug my phone into the car stereo and choose a worship song from a recently-released Bethel album. There is something about the song, as it begins playing, something I find is gripping me.

'Cause I loved you before you knew it was love
I saw it all, still I chose the cross
You were the one that I was thinking of
When I rose from the grave
Now rid of the shackles, My victory is yours
I tore the veil for you to come close
There's no reason to stand at a distance anymore
You're not far from home [4]

Whatever this is, it's so small, so very slight. So small that it is almost as if it is not even there—but it is. I am beginning to feel . . . something. I am not sure what it is. I have not felt anything for months. I can't even remember the last time I felt this way. I don't know how to describe it—I feel a presence I had long forgotten. The slightest drawing I chose to push away a long time ago. I feel a love I had thrown away, a quiet beckoning and call. I quickly hit the power button on my car's sound system. I don't like what is happening in me. It is scaring me—feelings that I can't be in control of. I know if I allow myself to feel anything at all then everything I have been pushing down will come rushing up all at once, and I am certain I could not handle that.

That presence that has invaded my car will not leave, despite me shutting off the music and driving the remainder of the way in silence. It continues to stay, calling me,

---

4   *Out of Hiding (Father's Song)* by Steffany Gretzinger and Amanda Cook. Copyright © 2014 Bethel Music Publishing

drawing me to come. Though Casey is not on my mind, and my plans have not changed to continue to leave him and finish the divorce, that nagging question that began in the back of my mind three days ago is now at the forefront of my thoughts. Was. It. Me. I've been unsuccessful in trying to get it out of my head. It is making me ponder things I don't want to think about.

As much as I do not want to admit it, something in me has changed—not what I thought would change, not the closure I expected to have before I came to Restoring the Foundations. Even though I am unsure of what exactly has shifted, I know I am not returning to Hamilton as the same person who left.

Chapter 22

WORDS

Word curses. What exactly are they? What do they mean? How do they happen? And most importantly, how do we cast them off or prevent them from landing? Most of us will have grown up saying or hearing the well-known statement, "Sticks and stones may break my bones but words can never hurt me." Oh, how we wished that statement were true in the midst of being heartbroken at something someone said about or to us. Words hurt—no two ways about it. We live up to them even when we say we don't. Likewise, through us, words kill; they label who others are.

Proverbs 18:21 (The Message) says that, "Words kill, words give life; they're either poison or fruit—you choose." Word curses are just that: poison. They are poison to our lives, they are poison to others. It's amazing how such a little thing as a curse can cause so much damage. It is easy to believe that words have no effect, especially when we are saying things to or about others. We are given a choice:

we can speak life, or we can speak death—but it is *our* choice, and that choice can come with lifelong blessings or consequences that we will live with, even when we say something about another.

Why is your husband lazy? Why is your wife dramatic and immature? Why are your kids rebellious? Why is there strife in your home? Why is your boss unreasonable and stupid? Could it be because we have poisoned these people with our words? Have you noticed how we use statements like "I am the way I am because of what my father said about me as a child" or "I battle with insecurity because of how my old relationships talked to me." Are those things true? Absolutely. But what we don't realize, or choose not to realize, rather, is that the problems in others could be our own fault, because of what we have spoken over them.

Do we talk about our husbands and say anything like "Why is he so lazy? He can't do anything. He just lays around like a lump on a log. He's like raising another child"? Are things said to or about wives like, "You always overreact. You're overweight. You never listen. Why don't you get off my back"? Have we said to our children, "You're never going to be anything. You are so rebellious. Stop being immature. Stop acting stupid"? How can we sit around and wonder why our husbands, wives, and children are the way they are? They are that way because we made them so! The good news is, we can change it.

What would change in your home if you went to your

husband and said, "You're really incredible at what you do, and I really appreciate you getting up and going to work and providing for us." You may be saying in your mind, "My husband is not like that." But could he be? Would it be possible to so believe something and then speak it into existence so that it becomes reality? Could it be because he was so spoken down to that he has spent years living up to those negative statements? After all, nothing else has ever been expected of him.

What would change if we changed our words? Chances are, your husband would pretty quickly be all in at work, coming home with pride, with his head held high, because he knows his wife is proud of and appreciates him. How could this happen? Because life has been spoken over something that was dead. What would happen to our children if they heard, "Sweetie, you are brilliant. You're so smart, and I am so proud of you." In reality their reaction will probably be something like, "Yeah thanks, whatever, Mom"! But what are we doing? We're speaking life into them. What they do not see is that tiny spark of life we just spoke into their heart and mind. What would happen if you looked at your wife and said, "You're so beautiful, and you work so hard"? You may not see anything right away, but water has been given to dry and dead soil.

When we gossip, slander, and speak death over ourselves or others, we are standing in the line of fire for the judgment of God in our own lives. This is explained in Matthew 7:1-2 (AMP): "Do not judge and criticize and condemn [others unfairly with an attitude of self-righteous superiority as though assuming the office of a judge], so that you will not be judged [unfairly]. For just as you [hypocritically] judge others [when you are sinful and unrepentant], so will you be judged; and in accordance with your standard of measure [used to pass out judgment], judgment will be measured to you."

Not only will we be judged for the same things, but also we will be judged with the same severity with which we have judged. That is a frightening thought. Let's break this down a bit more.

When we hear "don't judge and criticize and condemn" we often do not think it applies to us. But if we look at what these words actually mean it is a bit easier to see how they have been used in or through us.

- **To judge:** to form an opinion or conclusion about; to view, deem, pronounce, decree, rule; to assess or evaluate.
- **To criticize:** to indicate the faults of someone or something in a disapproving way; form and express a sophisticated judgment of; to rail against; to take apart, pull apart, pummel, trash or nitpick.
- **To condemn:** to express complete disapproval of, typically in public; to sentence someone to a particular punishment; prove or show guilt of; to find fault in, convict, blame, berate, doom.

If we apply these definitions to a situation in our lives, and take just one of the meanings of those words and apply it to the verse above, it reads very differently:

"Lindsey, when you are talking to or about Casey, do not form an opinion about, decree, view, or evaluate him. Do not indicate his faults, rail against, pull him apart, or trash him. Do not express disapproval of him; sentence him, convict, or blame him, for just as you form a conclusion about, pummel, or berate him, it will be done to you. And with the same measure you passed out opinions and conclusions it will be measured to you."

This shines a whole new light on the power of our words. It changes everything about what we say, and even think about the people in our lives. Now let's take this full circle and realize how easy it is to speak death over others; and also realize the power those words hold and what they can make happen. It is a terrifying thought.

Is there any good news to this? Yes. In the same way we have the power to speak word curses and death, we have the power to speak life. We have everything we need to change those words, to change the circumstances in our lives—and with nothing more than what comes out of our mouths. It is easy to believe we can heal the sick, raise the dead, and perform miracles with "the power of our words" because, after all, the Word says in Mark 11:23 that if you speak to the mountain it will be cast into the sea. It is easy to shout and dance and sing over things we really want to see change.

You don't have to be stiff and cold with no pulse to be dead. What is dead in our lives right now? Our marriage, our job, our finances, our children? We have the power to speak and change those circumstances! So why don't we? Even over our own lives. Why don't we change our fate? Speak it! Do it! And it can be so. Go ahead and try right now, as you are reading this. In fact, I will do it over my own family with you.

My daughter, Analeise, is loving and kind. She makes wise decisions. She is everything God wants her to be. I am proud of everything she is and will become. Analeise loves the Word of God. She is hungry for more of who God is every day. Analeise is blessed with godly influences and friends. She is beautiful inside and out, and radiates the glory of God everywhere she goes.

My daughter Katie is joyful and compassionate. She loves to love people and make people smile. Katie has a brilliant mind. She is creative and artistic. Katie is stunningly beautiful and pure. She is passionate, and chases the Lord and His presence. Katie uses wisdom in all her choices. She listens to the voice of God and no other voice will she follow.

My son Asher is a man of God. He is pure in thought and action. He is happy. He is blessed. Asher is going to walk in the will of God for his life. He will be kind and gentle, but strong. He will be everything he is meant to be. He will know no lack. Asher will speak wisdom. He will love to live life and will live it fully.

My husband Casey is blessed. He is wise. Casey is a passionate father and husband. He loves his children and walks in wisdom as their father. Casey hears the voice of God clearly. He is confident and content in who he is in the Lord. Casey is a provider, and protector. He is honored, and respected. Casey is loved everywhere he goes.

What is it about these words that make them different from prayers? It is that they are not questions, they are not petitions. They are statements, declarations. I am not *asking* for those things to happen—I am *speaking* them out in faith. I am choosing to speak them into existence. I am speaking life over my family and my home. Sometimes these words are spoken to them directly. Sometimes they are spoken as I fold their laundry and think about them. Sometimes it is spoken when Analeise or Katie have their feelings hurt and need to be reminded of who God says they are.

When we are speaking things over people it is important to note that we only speak according to the will and Word of God. Nothing is spoken to try and manipulate anything toward what we want. Speak according to His Word and His will and things will change. Likewise, speak death or poison and things will change too—but not for the better.

If you have found yourself in need of having words broken off of you, I encourage you to take those things to the feet of Jesus. You have the power to break them off of you and to speak life over yourself as well. The enemy will still bring up thoughts about yourself—thoughts and memories of what people have said. In those moments, counter the thoughts with what God believes and says about you. For example, "Lindsey, you're a victim, and you'll never be any different"—that thought, as small as it is, can have massive consequences if believed and acted upon. Now I have a choice. I can let the thought take root—or I can fight back: "I am not a victim. I walk in humility, ownership, and with a repentant heart." When you need to counter something said about you, or to break off labels you have grown up with, listen to what God says about you. What does His Word say about who you are and who He wants you to be?

If you need to repent for a word curse spoken over another, I encourage you to go to God for it and to bless that person instead. It doesn't always have to be someone in our families. It could be a co-worker, it could be a boss, or it could be someone we casually gossiped about over coffee with a friend. Whoever it is, break the word curses off of them and speak life back over them. You have the power to do that—and the power for it is in your words.

Chapter 23

HE'S SPEAKING

"Lindsey . . . Lindsey . . ."

I hear a voice whispering to me, pulling me back into reality.

"Pssst. Lindsey."

A slight nudge to my arm snaps me out of my daydream. Dianne, my attorney, is trying to get my attention. I find myself back in the courtroom. I have day-dreamed this whole mediation away. I am pulled back to this wretched November day. In the past couple of hours, while our attorneys have been debating and arguing back and forth and recording the final settlement, I have relived the whole past two years. I shake my head as if coming out of a dream.

"Yes?" I quickly reply back to her.

"Is there anything you would like to add to or say in this final mediation recording?" I don't even know what is on the recording. What I do know is I have become a hard, numb, dark woman. Although my trip to North Carolina with Ashley was over a month ago, I still fight those questions and feelings I left there with—especially in the moments I have to see Casey face-to-face. I have them when I look into the eyes of my two girls.

"Oh, um . . . no. I think that settles everything," I finally reply. My attorney nods and smiles at me. It's finally over. After two years of meetings, mediations, papers, and negotiations back and forth, it's over. The attorneys shake hands. The mediator says his final closing remarks and leaves the room. I glance over at Casey quickly and discreetly so I will not be caught, but he is not looking anyway. He looks relieved almost. Surely not? I try to convince myself I am relieved as well—but if I am totally honest, I'm not. I don't regret it per se, but I'm not happy about it either.

I can go on with my life now. It's not like I haven't gone on with my life already but now it's legal. I am bound to no one. Casey can go on with his life, too. He will probably find himself that trophy wife now, someone he won't be embarrassed by, someone who will worship the ground he walks on. But, she won't know how he likes his Pepsi, or how he twists his hair when he's tired. She won't know him at all. Well, heck if I care. He can do whatever he wants now. Although I don't want to admit it, the thought of him being able to move on and find someone else to love and who will love him really bothers me. Did I really hate him so much? It doesn't feel like that now. It does not feel like love either, though. I'm not sure what this feeling is. Maybe it's just the nerves. As I watch Casey walk out of the room and to his car that same question that haunted me in North Carolina comes right back up: Was this me?

It is dark, and my Florence apartment is chilly when I walk in. I quickly drop my bag and throw on my plush, warm robe. Logan wanted to come by tonight but I am not up for company. Instead I decide to sit alone and binge-watch the first season of my favorite show, *Once Upon a Time*. I have seen these episodes multiple times— so much so that I can probably quote most of this season. I catch my heart starting to pound harder and a lump form in my throat as the lead character spins the wedding band on her finger, as she watched the love of her life live his life with another—and there is nothing she can do about it. Nothing, but live in the pain and misery of being alone while the person she really loves moves on, just beyond her reach. She had him, and due to a curse, she lost him. Lost him to another. That is exactly what will happen to me. I see my whole life play out ahead of me. Casey will go on. He will be happy. He will become everything God wanted him to become, but he won't do it with me. I, on the other hand, will be alone, continuing to go through a string of men, one after another, after another, never being satisfied. I will end up working some random job that will just put food on the table. I will never have my company, my school. My beautiful dream is gone, burnt to ash. There is nothing for me to keep living for, save my two girls.

They are the only two glimmers of light in the black hole of my life. But I know one day they will discover the truth about the divorce, and when that day comes they will want to know the answers to all the questions. I will either have to continue the lie, stretching it larger and larger or tell them the truth. That truth however will turn them against me. They will never forgive me for leaving their daddy and they will never believe me if I lie to them.

Life has lost all joy now. Even the tension of the divorce proceedings, though horrible, at least provided some form of activity to my life. Now that everything is over there is nothing. Nothing but the memories. Nothing but the regret.

Over the next month my dimly-colored life turns completely gray. Despite Christmas, saying goodbye to 2015, and welcoming a new and fresh year, I am sadder than ever. People from the church ask for me and the girls to join them at lunch or for coffee, but it's becoming a burden to go. They are wonderful people, kind people, and I know they really want to help and love me, but putting on the fake smile only lasts so long and now I am tired of putting it on. The friends that took my side in the divorce are rejoicing, texting and calling, thrilled that everything is over. Daddy and Joyce are gloriously happy. I am finally free . . . yeah . . . free to live exactly the life I asked for. Freedom . . . it came at a high price, and it doesn't feel free at all. My life is a grave, it is never satisfied.

Nothing scratches the itch. Nothing meets the need. I have become a master at going through the motions and making the facial expressions of a strong, passionate, "no one can mess with me and get away with it" woman. But it is nothing more than a mask. No one knows I am dying inside and I will never tell.

I have spent the last few weeks stalking Casey on social media. Though he has not moved on with anyone romantically, his life has moved on. He looks happy. He is happy, and he doesn't have to fake it. He has his friends in his pictures: real friends—friends that didn't use him for their own benefit and motives. He is secure, stable. He is free, truly free, and I am the one who is bound. He has lost so much weight from the stress of the past two years, but he is still quite handsome. He still has those piercing dark blue eyes and our daughter Analeise's light golden brown hair. He still has those high, chiseled cheekbones and thick, broad lips. They were the first things I noticed when I first met him fifteen years ago. They are still as attractive to me now as they were then. Some things will never change.

Though Logan has kept me company these past months, our relationship has just added another link to the chain of bondage and misery I feel growing every day. I ended everything with him a day or so ago. Counterfeit affection will never meet that need deep inside of me—I am learning that more and more. I didn't want to hurt the guy and I never meant to, but he was far more involved and invested in the relationship than I was. I couldn't keep him on a string with hopes of us being something we were never going to be. Now he becomes another name I can add to my list of casualties. Another person I shattered. I truly have become a monster.

Laying in bed on a cold January night I decide to open my Bible. I've not cracked it open since . . . well, I don't really know since when. It has been too long to remember now. Opening it to Luke 15, I begin to read.

A certain man had two sons. And the younger of them said to his father, "Father, give me the portion of goods that falls to me." So he divided to them his livelihood. And not many days after, the younger son gathered all together, journeyed to a far country, and there wasted his possessions with prodigal living. But when he had spent all, there arose a severe famine in that land, and he began to be in want. Then he went and joined himself to a citizen of that country, and he sent him into his fields to feed swine. And he would gladly have filled his stomach with the pods that the swine ate, and no one gave him anything. But when he came to himself, he said, "How many of my father's hired servants have bread enough to spare, and I perish with hunger! I will arise and go to my father, and will say to him, 'Father, I have sinned against heaven and before you, and I am no longer worthy to be called your son. Make me like one of your hired servants.'"
Luke 15:11-19, NKJV

He is right. The life of a servant in the house of my family would be far better than what the current situation is. They have joy enough to spare, freedom enough to spare, and here I am dying. Starving to death. Not for bread or meat, but for truth and love and hope. I am desperately hungry to be healed and whole, though I denied it before. Desperate to be happy. But I have been given over to the life I chose and the consequences of that life. I deserve to suffer. I deserve this pain. Why did I give up all I had for this? The most challenging days in my marriage exceed this life by far. But I chose this. I wanted this. And I got exactly the cards I dealt.

Finally the answer to the question I have had for the past month dawns on me. I *do* know the answer. Perhaps I have always known it, and that's why I have been so tormented.

I am fighting against God and myself.

This WAS me. I did this.

This was my fault, and now I have gone too far, pushed them all too far. I am the prodigal, and I chose a life with the swine. That night I dreamt of the life I could have had, of everything I gave up. Casey, my girls, they are just beyond my reach. I call out to them but the sound stops just short of my lips. I am screaming silently. Darkness is overtaking me body and soul.

Chapter 24

THE PIGPEN ALWAYS WORKS

I wake long before the alarm goes off on my phone. Church begins in two hours, but today something is different. Very different. That "something" I've been feeling in me since the Restoring the Foundations retreat is beginning to bloom.

The cold, January sunlight is streaming onto the foot of my bed. I crawl over to it and sit in that small stream, taking in its warmth from the cold that has, for a long time, been coming from within. Looking around my simply decorated room I wonder, "What am I doing here? What was I thinking?" The weight of my decisions hits me. This really was all my fault. I had everything I ever wanted and I gave it up. More than anything in the world I wanted to be happy. I could have had happiness, too. I could have had love. Real love. The kind everyone hopes is real and not just what you read about in stories; love that fights for you, love that keeps coming even when you try to push it away, love that looks like the sacrificial love of Christ. I could have had love that forgives, and is patient and kind; that defends you and forgives and…

Wait . . . it was Casey.

Casey was that love.

All the things he has done over the past several years come flooding over me: him tending to me when I was ill while I pushed him away so as to harden his heart so he'd leave me; him protecting me from gossip and rumors even when what people were saying about me was true; him sending me flowers on the day I wounded him the most; him never saying a bad word about me to a soul, even when I tried to obliterate his name and reputation. The countless hours he cried and prayed for me. I flaunted other men in his face, wanting to cut him as deeply as possible, while he remained completely faithful to me, even during the time we were separated.

What have I done? He is everything I have ever wanted! Would he even take me back now if I tried? I would, under no circumstances, deserve it. I would not take me back if I were him. Is he still fighting for me? Would he even want me to come home?

The divorce is over—all but the finality of the judge's signature, at least. Is he relieved? Is he sad? Does he still want me? Even if he does, he won't want someone who has done far more than he currently knows about. He doesn't know about that night with August. No one does.

What would he do if I told him? He doesn't know I gave my heart away to Tristan. I never actually admitted it to him.

I begin to weigh all of my options. I know whatever decision I make will have massive repercussions. I've spent the last few weeks missing my family and home terribly, but more than anything in the world, more than anyone, I miss him. I miss Casey. I miss us being a family. Everything I remember about our life together is rushing though my mind: what he looked like when he first woke up and had bed head, the way his arm felt around me when he kissed me, how he crossed his ankles when he propped up his feet, the sound of his Pepsi cans opening. I remember his tear-filled eyes as he looked at our newborn daughters, how he tucked them in at night. I suddenly remember the lines in his face as he smiles. His dimples, the sound of his laugh. Is it too late? What will he say if I tell him I want to come home?

Oh God, what would Daddy say? He will be so upset with me if I choose to go back home. With mediation behind us he has been looking forward to me being on my own. We talk every day, even if it is just to say hello. I will lose him. I will lose Joyce. For the first time in my life I felt like I had that father-daughter relationship I'd always wanted. But any relationship formed out of offense is toxic, and it will come crashing down sooner or later anyway. If I go home it will be the nail in the coffin of a long-damaged relationship between him and me. My stepsister, stepbrother, all their children who call me Aunt Lindsey—I will lose them all, probably permanently. But I've lied to them, too. I used them as my way out. I took advantage of their offense. Everything is a lie, and to continue to lie and use them would be wrong. Even if they never forgive me, at least they will know the truth. I will always love them. Always. He's my father and though I know what this will cost our relationship, I can't continue to lie to him taking advantage of his support, time, and money. I am wrong for what I did to him and Joyce. Had I not been so desperate to have my own dreams, have my own freedom and lied to them to begin with, we would never be here. We would probably still be able to have a relationship today. Deception truly painted a different picture for me than this, and my own actions will cost me my father and step-mother. God, please forgive me for what I did to them, for the lies I told them.

I think of all the relationships I have built at the church where I live now: the pastors, worship leaders, youth pastors, and friends. I have lied to them, too. I've lied to all of them, and none of it was intentional. I really did believe all those terrible things about my marriage I'd told myself. I wanted them to be true so badly, so I could have my happiness and freedom, I was willing to believe and spread whatever I had to.

My old dreams of being a dancer and choreographer will be gone. I will never have the studio. I will never have the school. I will never have the theater company. I will have to give it up forever. I abused the right to have a dance career. I broke trust. To my surprise, the more I weigh my options, the more willing I am to give it all up.

Going back means I will have to face all the people I lied to and somehow try to make it right. I will have to face our church where Casey is still a pastor. As a pastor's wife I will have to get up and expose where I was wrong and hope I will receive at least some level of mercy. All those eyes, all the judgment they will hold. I was wrong about all of it. I was wrong about the ministry. I willingly believed wrong about them. They protected and shielded me, even when I lied and spread rumors, saying they were a cult and only out to protect themselves and their own name. I was a fool—an absolute fool.

I will have to face my mom, my sister, and my brother-in-law Sam. Even he tried to reach out and love me during the past two years, and I shoved him away. What will they say? "I told you so, Lindsey, I told you. Now you've screwed things up and you want to come home? Now? Of all times! You expect us to just let you walk back into our lives?" God knows, I would deserve that. Because they would be right. I believed the absolute worst of all of them. Other than Casey, I tried to hurt my mother the worst. I hated her for taking Casey's side. Now I see that was a lie, too—because Casey was not wrong, I was. Mom was siding with the truth; even when I yelled at her, threw things at her, cut her off, took advantage of her, she still stood for truth. She loved me, still called me to talk, still took me out to spend time with me, still bought me dinner, still protected and loved me—while all the time she took every bullet I shot at her.

I will have to face Casey's family. His mother Pam, his sister Hadassah, his niece and nephew, aunts and uncles—they will never forgive me. Never. They will never trust me again. Who could blame them? I tore Casey apart, piece by piece. They could forever be in his ear telling him it's a bad idea, telling him not to take the chance—and they would have every right to. I gave them every right to.

I think of all the ministers I will have to face. Men and women of God I have known my whole life. Pastors Rusty, Randy, Judy, Jamie, Eddie, all of them. I lied to them all. They tried to help me. They loved me. They wanted what was really best for me, and I lied to them. I lied and played the victim when they didn't say what I wanted to hear. I've disappointed them all. Hurt them all. These are men and women who have prayed and prayed for me—what will they think?

There has been so much damage done. I can't fix it all. I am looking at a shattered, broken, and burned city, holding nothing but a screwdriver. All the people I've disappointed, all the people who will have questions that I will have to answer. I am so unbelievably ashamed. How did I let myself become this way? How did I get so far away from the truth? How did I run so far, so fast? My God, how did this happen? How did I lose that little girl in me who loves so deeply and can't stand to see anyone hurting? How did I lose her? How did I lose me? If nothing else, I have to at least say I'm sorry. I have to at least repent of what I have done. None of them have to forgive me, and I don't deserve forgiveness anyway. But I have to try to make it right. I do not deserve grace, not even a little bit, not an ounce. But they deserve an apology. They deserve much more than that in reality but, at the very least, I can give them that much.

What are my other options in all of this? I can stay where I am. I can continue to live in Florence. I can see Casey move on with his life and I will move on with mine. I can work a job and come home to whoever is the latest in my string of guys. I can live in regret, self-pity, and bitterness, never knowing what would have happened if I had just tried. Really tried. I wonder what could have been if I had given our marriage 100 per cent. What would life look like in five, ten, or even forty years from now?

I look up, as if I am looking past my ceiling, past the sky and stars, into the very face of God. My mind is made up. I have made my choice. I don't want to dance. I don't want to choreograph. I don't want any of my new friends. I don't want this wretched life I made for myself! Dear God, I just want everything to be right! I just want to know the truth again. I know what it will cost me, and I will gladly pay it. I know what people will say, and I don't care. Truth is far more important to me than any opinion some will have of me. Dear God, please, please forgive me for what I have done. I deserve judgment, every bit of it.

I don't deserve to be forgiven or loved by any of them again. But please, PLEASE, give me the chance to say I'm sorry even if they don't accept me back.

Sitting in that stream of bright sunlight I finally admit it, even to myself: I want Casey. I miss him. I miss him so bad. If he asked me to—no, even if he doesn't ask me to—I'll give it all up. I will prove to him that I will give it all up. I just want him. I want my girls. I want my family back. I want my home and, more than all of it, I want him. I love him. I've always loved him. I will always love him.

I look up through the sunlight. "God!" I cry out. "God . . . my answer is yes."

The very second I decide to open my heart back up to love and to life, a peace I cannot describe without using spiritual tongues washes over me. There is no doubt God is with me and is backing my every move. Though I do not know what this path will look like, and though I do not know how long it will take, I am taking this road. People can mock me, they can judge me, they can hate me, I'm still saying yes. I am still going to try. I don't care if Casey says no to me. I will keep trying until he says yes. I don't care how long it takes, I will keep trying even if it takes the rest of my life. I don't care if I have to sleep on his porch or in his yard. I will lay my head in his grass until he says yes. If he moves away, then I will go too, and I will never stop trying.

This is going to be the hardest road I have ever walked,

but, come hell or high water, I have made my decision . . .

I'm going home.

Chapter 25

REPENTANCE (THE PIGPEN EXAMPLE)

Before we move on to finish the rest of my story, I want us to look back over the story of The Prodigal Son for a moment. In Luke 15:15-16 (NLT) we read: "He persuaded a local farmer to hire him, and the man sent him into his fields to feed the pigs. The young man became so hungry that even the pods he was feeding the pigs looked good to him. But no one gave him anything."

There is a statement we frequently use in our house: "The pigpen always works."

Not only is the prodigal son away from the house of his father, he is working for a Gentile, and, if that weren't bad enough, he was a Jew living among swine, the most unclean and untouchable animal. He found himself at the very lowest point he could have been. The only place lower for him would have been a grave. The "pigpen" moment is necessary for any radical turn around in a person's life. It is difficult, if not impossible, to have a true-blue moment of repentance if you have not had that rock bottom, pigpen moment. Until that moment comes, our actions are still justifiable and our lifestyles are not that bad. We are still able to make excuses for them. We are still able to keep on living, but eventually the consequences of our life choices will catch up to us.

Once Upon a Time is a popular TV series with a simple reoccurring phrase: "Magic always comes with a price." The characters in this show frequently request magic for dire circumstances or desires, but they are always warned that, "Magic comes with a price." What they don't realize is the price they pay comes with pain, trauma, loss of relationships, darkness, and sometimes death. Some of their choices are reversible, and they are able to fix their mistakes, but most cannot be undone, and they are forced to live with their choices. Sin works in the same way. It ALWAYS comes with a price, and it is a much higher price than we expect to pay.

As Christians we frequently throw around the term "sin" or "sinning" lightly. When we hear those terms, most of us picture some radical act of darkness. We picture in our minds the drug-addicted homeless person who has yet to find a merciful God, or we see the selfish, cruel, power-hungry person, or the atheist who denies the very existence of God. Of course, none of us are really "sinners". Yes, at occasional points in the past we have sinned, but for the most part we are all good people, doing good things, and the things that are not so good in our lives, well, they are totally normal, especially in today's culture and society. After all, the Bible is changeable with today's culture, right? That's why we can justify abortion, adultery, divorce, homosexuality—because to us it's "normal." It is why we can justify what we allow our kids to watch, say, and do. It's just a part of the changing of the times. We don't use bad language—at least not too bad. We don't spend night after night in a bar. We don't go all the way into the affair, we just have feelings in our hearts. We are not addicted to pornography, we just look at a picture every once in a while. But sin is sin. Sin is timeless. It doesn't change and neither do the consequences of sin. It is not less of a sin today than it was a thousand years ago, when culture was different.

The Word of God is unchangeable. We don't get to take out the Bible verses that discuss homosexuality because it offends today's generation. Those verses are law that applies to a much bigger court room than any we face on this earth, and the Judge we will face in that room has the power to judge not for five, ten, or twenty years, not even for a lifetime sentence, but for an eternity.

How dare we justify our actions and the actions of others just because they or we are "good people"? Being good does not give you automatic immunity from the consequences of our actions. In this life it doesn't matter how good you are: if you rob a bank you go to jail, regardless of all the good you've done prior. You could be the best person in the world and still break the law of heaven. You could hide every sin you've ever done and no one around you would ever know. But there is a God who knows, and there will be a sentencing for the breaking of that law. It could be something as major as murder or as simple as a little white lie. The Word is absolute and unchanging and He who wrote it is just. This is not to frighten us. It is not to say "there is a big eye in the sky waiting to squash you like a bug when you sin." It is to make us aware of how easy it is to justify the little sins in our lives, and those little unnoticeable sins will most assuredly grow to become life-altering decisions if not dealt with.

Sin sneaks up on us when we don't expect it. It takes root, grows, and eventually consumes like a parasite. It is the silent killer. Sin has an uncanny way of catching up to us. This is why you hear of countless ministers who tragically fall after getting caught cheating on their spouses, and lose everything. Did they wake up one day and say, "Oh, I think today I will have an affair. Yeah, that's a great plan." No! It was the tiniest of sins, one that was undetectable as even being a sin that started the affair in motion. It was the look across the room that led to the text that led to the phone call that led to the counseling session that led to the secret meeting that led to the hug and kiss that led to an entire evening together. Once we give in to darkness it's almost impossible to resist its call. It lures us in, looking like everything we have ever wanted. When we fall from those moments, we fall fast and we fall hard. It is only when we have lost everything that the enemy pulls back the curtain and mocks us in glee. He has won. We took the bait. We never saw the hook, we bit and we bit hard. We have hit rock bottom. Now we lie dying, starving, exposed, humiliated, and ashamed. Now, after it is too late, we come to our senses. But now we have a choice to make.

Like sin, repentance is another word taken lightly within the Christian world. Generally we see it as a pretty word for "I'm sorry", but that is NOT it at all. The definition of the word "repent" is "to turn from sin and dedicate oneself to the amendment of one's life." Repentance is not an apology, because an apology can be followed by a repeat offense. Repentance is a complete 180-degree turnaround from one's actions and lifestyle. It is a commitment and an action you take to never do and live that way again.

The Beatitudes are not generally scriptures we look to as a reference for repentance. We kind of, sort of, look at a couple of them for funerals, or for people going through a life tragedy. You know, "Blessed are the mournful for they shall be comforted," etc. But what was the picture Jesus was trying to paint on that mountain, as described in Matthew, chapter 5?

God blesses those who are broken in spirit and realize their need for Him, for the kingdom of Heaven is theirs.
Matthew 5:3

The biblical picture of this moment is that of a beggar begging for a crumb of bread. It means to come to the end of yourself, to see the true condition of your soul, to see your impoverished condition before God. It is the moment you have hit rock bottom and have nowhere else to go.

God blesses those who mourn, for they will be comforted.
Matthew 5:4

It is here where we find our moments of remorse, sorrow, and grief. We have finally realized the state of our condition before God. We have seen and are in shock and shame of where we are and what we have become. How could we have gotten here? How did it get this bad? This was not the end result we were looking for. Look at what we have become! We begin to grieve over the condition of our choices, our lives, and, sadly, what we have lost. It is easy to stay in this place. After all, now, we deserve nothing more than what we asked for—and this is what we have asked for. But to stay here it is NOT what God wants for us.

God blesses those who are humble, for they will
inherit the whole earth.
Matthew 5:5

When we have found ourselves at rock bottom, where can we go? You already know the answer: Up. There is nowhere else to go but up. We can't get there through pride. We get there through humility. It is only after seeing our sin, after grief and mourning, that we can begin to crawl out of our dark pit. Now we look up and we do not see an angry Father, we see one who is looking earnestly down the road, running to us with open arms. Here is where we pour out our hearts, our souls, in the realization of how small we truly are in the midst of a great big God. But true repentance takes true humility. It takes honesty, vulnerability, and extreme ownership. It means making NO defense or excuse for our actions. After all, once we find ourselves in the pigpen, we don't want to offer any excuse: we finally see the truth.

God blesses those who hunger and thirst for justice,
for they will be satisfied.
Matthew 5:6

To be righteous, to be free of guilt and sin—can you imagine a life like that? A life utterly free of sin. Is it possible? Yes. Is it possible on this side of heaven? Yes. Now, don't start thinking in terms of a theology that says, "We can no longer sin." As long as we have a free will, we are capable of sinning.

However, it is absolutely possible to make such a radical turnaround, to run as hard and as fast as we can back toward truth—as much as we did toward destruction—that what we fought before will never be an issue in our lives again. Not because it magically just went away, but because we are so dead set, so resolved, to never ever go back that we never again allow even the thought of our past temptations and sins to cross our minds. It takes a radical commitment to go there, a willingness to do WHATEVER IT TAKES to never go back. It means cutting off ANYONE AND ANYTHING that could be a trigger to those past sins. Why is it that a drug addict can go through rehab, be clean for months, or even sometimes years, and then see or smell something that reminds them of their past life, and they fall head-long back into the addictive lifestyle? It was a trigger, as simple as that. Something set them off and sent them back. For them to be truly free, they have to cut off all those triggers. They have to burn all the bridges.

For you, it may mean never speaking to a best friend or even a family member ever again. Could they repent and the two of you restore the relationship? Perhaps, but if they did not, would you be willing to cut them off in order to be free? It may mean never having a computer in your house ever again, never watching certain movies or listening to certain music ever again. It is so easy to think we will be strong enough to just say no to those things, that we could still be around those people and hold to our new convictions. Wrong. We are dead wrong when we think that way. If that were possible, we would never have fallen in the first place. How hungry are you for righteousness? How bad do you want to be clean and right before God?

> *God blesses those who are merciful for they will be*
> *shown mercy. God blesses those whose hearts are*
> *pure, for they will see God.*
> **Matthew 5:7-8**

We will look at these last two together. When we have finally made it down the road of repentance, we now have a new responsibility. How easy it is to turn around and point the finger at others who are going through EXACTLY what we just walked out of. How easy it is to cast judgment and condemnation on them. Shame on us for doing such things! Shame on us for showing judgment, when we were given such mercy when we were begging for that crumb from the table. Now is not the time to cast our own verdicts as if we were the judges. Now is the time to show another how to walk out of the fire. Those coming behind you need your road. Please, do not block that road with judgment. Mercy is the last step before we get to the most glorious reward of all: pure hearts. It is then, and only then, we can see our glorious Father. We are not given access to see Him until our hearts are pure; and to be pure, we must be truly repentant. We have to take ownership. But what joy, what peace there is, what unspeakable peace to know this: I walk in repentance, righteousness, mercy, and purity before my Father. Such a simple concept, but what a reward.

Repentance requires radical changes. It is no easy road. It is so much more than a prayer at the altar. It is more than falling down in the Spirit, speaking in tongues, or even prophesying. It is more than being able to lay hands on and pray for others. All of those things can be done while we still go home and live in our sins.

Repentance doesn't have to be at an altar. It can be right now in your room, sitting on an airplane, at a ball game, anywhere. It can be the simplest of prayers, just asking God to meet you where you are in that pigpen and to reach down His hand of mercy and allow you to come back into His arms. It is then taking any action necessary to never, never, never go back. No matter what, no matter the cost. Never. Going. Back.

Do not take repentance lightly. All sin comes with a price, and that price was paid for by the life of our Lord. He meant it when He said, "It is finished." Look the life you're living square in the eye and make that same commitment—it is finished.

Chapter 26

YOU'VE GOT MAIL

"Ashley. Please, I need your help." I text her as soon as I stand up from my spot at the end of my bed. I don't want anyone going to Casey before I can talk to him myself, so I know she is the only person I can tell and get counsel from regarding how to go about getting home.

"What's wrong?" she immediately texts back.

"Ash . . . I miss him."

"You miss who?"

"I miss Casey."

Immediately my phone rings. She is crying and laughing on the other end of the phone. Crying, laughing, praising God, crying more. I would join her but I am head-set; I need help and fast. The past two years felt like they took forever but all of a sudden I feel as if I have no time to reach Casey before it is too late.

"Ashley, I don't know what to do. How do I contact him? Texting would not be right, he deserves more than that. I can't show up in person 'cause he will probably tell me to leave, and would have every right to do it. WHAT DO I DO?" My urgency is quickly turning to panic. I have to calm down. She asks me the one question she knows will mean whether or not I am serious about this.

"Linds, you will probably never dance again. Would you be willing to give all of those dreams up?" She knows my dream of "freedom and happiness," and of having my own company and school, have been some of the driving forces behind everything. She has asked this before and every time my answer was no.

"I will give up everything to be with him, Ashley. Everything. All of it. Please help me. What do I do?"

She and Josh talk with me about different ways I could contact him. It is wonderful to have Josh's perspective, too, since he's a guy and knows how a man would view the different approaches. Finally, I decide an email would be best. It is more personal than a text but not quite as invasive as showing up at his door, especially when I have hurt him this much.

"Don't expect him to answer back, Lindsey," Josh says. "He is hurt. Deeply hurt. He may not answer back at all. Not ever."

"I understand." I know Josh is right, but even if Casey does not respond, I will still try, and I will email him again. Either way, I am still going to pack up my things and move back home—even if I have to live with Mom or my grandmother, or anyone for that matter. I will do anything to prove to him I want to come home and be with him.

I sit there and compose my email to him. It is hard to even know what to say, but I give it my best shot, expressing as much sincerity as possible, hoping and praying he will hear my heart, even though he will probably never respond back.

Dear Casey,
I made the worst mistake of my life divorcing you. I
have hurt everybody. I don't deserve a second
chance, but I would give up anything to have one. I
really can't explain everything that has happened.
But this morning I woke up missing you terribly. I
truly am sorry.

I stare at my email, reading it over and over again, debating on whether or not I should just show up at his house. I press 'send'. Now, there is nothing to do but wait.

Wait and pray.

I go on about my morning, half floating and half terrified. I stand, I sit, I pace around. I sit again.

Thirty minutes go by.

An hour.

Then another.

I keep checking my email to see if there is any response at all. Nothing. I continue to pray, to beg for God's forgiveness and mercy, for God to protect Casey, for him to give me a chance. Just one chance to look him in the eyes and say I am sorry. Suddenly my phone vibrates. It's an email, but I refuse to get my hopes up. I glance down. It's from him.

Lindsey,
I don't know what to tell you. To be honest I do not know if the marriage can be restored or not. Part of me wants to say I love you, come home. Then part of me wants to say 'do not ever speak to me again'. I don't know if there is hope or not. But I am willing to talk about it.

I am stunned. Thrilled. Scared. I want to run to him, but I know I can't. He answered, which is more than I could ever have hoped for.

I immediately call Ashley. I need advice on what to do now. "Ash . . . He responded."

"He did what?!" I hear Josh is the background. "That is a man of God!"

I decide to respond back in a simple email thanking him for agreeing to talk to me and that I love him. I can't stay here in Florence tonight. I want to be close to him even if it can't be at his house. Packing a bag I decide to stay at Mom's for a couple of days. There is plenty I need to say to her, too, and I want to go to her in person.

"Hey Mom, can I talk to you?" I say as she opens her door.

"Of course, sweetie," she says.

We sit at her dinner table and I take out my phone. I say nothing but hand her the email I sent to Casey. I don't want to show anyone his email back to me yet so I leave his out. She looks up at me through tear-filled eyes.

"I want to come home. I want to fix it," I tell her.

Tears begin to fall down her cheeks. She says nothing, but I know they are tears of joy. I also know there will be time for us to heal our relationship as well, but for now she is very focused on helping me take this path toward Casey. She knows the journey ahead of me is going to be a near-impossible one.

"How can I help you, sweetheart? What can I do?" she asks.

"Just . . . try to help it stay quiet for now. People are going to see me at his house when we meet to talk and I want to keep all the discussions and questions down to a minimum. Help me keep everything protected while we try to talk and see what we can do."

That night, for the first time in two years, I slept at peace. Hopefully, soon, I will have my chance to meet with him. I will have my chance to apologize to him.

The next day is the college football national championship. We are having several people over to Mom's to eat and watch it. Casey will be watching it at a friend's house. I was hoping he would be here, but really didn't expect him to come. Prior to the game starting I go and buy him a bag of mini Reese's cups and a case of Pepsi—his favorite snack. I leave them at his doorstep while he is picking the girls up from school with a simple note attached as well: "Have a great time tonight."

I want to say so much more but I know it is not the time. To my surprise I receive a simple "Thank you" on my phone not long after I dropped off the snack at his house.

Lauren, and my brother-in-law Sam, will be at Mom's for the game. I will have my chance to tell them what I am doing and that I am sorry. As soon as I see them walk in the door I feel myself start to crack. Pulling them into a side room I break down in tears before I can say anything.

"I'm sorry. I am trying to fix everything. I'm sorry." A pathetic apology, but it is all I manage to get out before I break down into sobs. I expect to receive some form of judgment and reservations from them. Instead, my sister's arms wrap around me. She is crying, too, and even Sam is tearing up.

"It's going to be ok, Lindsey. Everything will be ok. We love you. So much."

I don't deserve this. And I can't believe it is happening. I don't deserve any of it.

That night I decide to attempt to set up a meeting with Casey. I consider messaging him during the game to ask if he would be willing to meet now, but Ash and Josh gave me a good piece of advice to not come on too strong, but just to continue reaching out to him, of course, and to do it daily, taking it easy and not putting too much of a demand on him or overwhelming him.

It is the morning of January 12th. It's been two days now since I first emailed Casey. I can't wait any longer. I message him.

"Good morning, Case. I wanted to see if you would be willing for us to meet and talk sometime tonight. Mom will keep the girls so we can talk. They can spend the night with her."

In reality, I have not checked with her yet and have gone ahead and volunteered her for the job. But I know for certain she will be okay with it—thrilled, actually.

"What time?" is the message I get back.

"Can I be there around 9? Mom will pick the girls up from your house and bring them to hers," I reply.

"That's fine," he says.

There is nothing else, but I don't care. He is agreeing to talk to me.

Now the fear factor really starts to set in. When I am alone I am excited and giddy thinking about him. Although I have refused to allow my mind to go to the place of planning and dreaming of us together again, sometimes I can't help it. I picture us sitting on the porch together holding hands, cuddling on the couch with our favorite movie, playing games with the girls . . . I want this day to go by faster. Later this evening I have to make a trip back to Florence to get some of my personal items to keep at Mom's since I am planning to stay there as long as possible. Nothing in me wants to go back to that city, though. I hate it now. I hate everything that brings up the memory of my life without him. As quickly as possible I gather some more clothes, shoes, and books. I throw them into my car and head back to Hamilton. It is not long until I will face him again—about an hour and a half actually. My heart is pounding so hard it feels as if it will burst.

He will have every right to say no to me, and I fully expect him to do so. If I had to predict what restoration would look like, if I am fortunate enough for Casey to agree to moving toward it with me, I would guess we'd probably date for a long time, at least a year. I will have to win him over again and I will do whatever it takes to do just that—and I don't care how long it takes. My only problem is that I don't know what to say to him when I arrive. How do you apologize for all the wrong you've done to someone? This isn't like apologizing for hurting someone's feelings. This goes deeper than anyone could express in words. For him to forgive me—just forgive me, not even take me back yet—would be a huge step for anyone. Still, no one, not even Mom knows how far I have gone in the past two years. I will have to tell him. Nothing can stay hidden tonight. The truth may end it all for him, I know that. But he has to know everything. He deserves to know everything. To give him anything but the full truth would be wrong and far more hurtful to him. I will have to bare all. Oh God, help me get through this.

Ashley is the only person I talk to before going to his house. I will not have time to go back to Mom's before he and I meet and, to be honest, I want to be alone first, to think about what is going to happen. I don't want to see anyone else until after he and I talk.

"Will you and Josh pray for me tonight? Right now, actually. I am going to meet with him." I say to her on the phone.

"Of course, Linds. And listen, he is probably not going to say a lot to you tonight. He is really, really hurt. You have no defense to play. Tell him everything and take ownership for it. Don't defend it 'cause there is nothing to defend. You were wrong. You know that. And no matter how intense it gets, and it will get intense, do not leave that house. You stay and stick it out. The enemy is going to try to get inside your head. Don't let him. You can do this."

I pull up in front of the quaint, white cottage he is currently living in, but before I walk in I sit alone in my car. I am shaking all over. It's okay if he says no. He will probably say no. I deserve a no. But even then I am so determined to keep trying, despite anything he says, so I go ahead and assume this will not be our last meeting. There will be several of these, and they will be hard. Brutal, even. But he is more than worth it. I have to be honest with myself and not get my hopes up. He is going to say no, and I will try again. I step out of my car and walk across his front lawn—it is the longest walk of my life.

He is going to say no, and I will try again. I walk up the small brick stairs to his porch, go to his door and knock. It is as if a boa constrictor has squeezed all the air out of my lungs as I wait for an answer. He is going to say no, and I will try again. The few seconds it takes feels like an eternity. I am shaking from head to toe. Finally I hear something. His footsteps are coming closer to where I am. The handle turns and there he is.

"Come in."

Chapter 27

DON'T LEAVE

My legs are suddenly like Jell-O and my feet like lead. It takes all I have in me to be able to walk in and sit in his living room. He takes a seat on the opposite end of the couch. He is hurting so much, and I am the cause of all of it. The lump in my throat is choking me. All at once, the years of pent-up emotion come pouring out. I want to erase time. Go back. Change everything. I can't. I made my choice and the consequences are all staring me in the face. My shoulders begin to shake with sobs.

"I am sorry, Casey. I am so sorry."

That's all that comes out. I want to say so much more to him, to tell him I love him more than anything in the world: to lie at his feet and beg for forgiveness. I want to take his face and kiss him. Hold him. Anything.

"Just answer me this, Lindsey, why did you do this to us? To the girls? Why?" His voice is so solemn. Not angry or mean, even, though I would deserve it if it were.

"I have no excuse. None. I was angry . . . and influenced by so many, but even the influence is no excuse. I should never have left you, Casey. It was the worst mistake of my life."

"You lied about me, Lindsey. You said I abused you. What am I supposed to do with that? You knew that wasn't true when you said it. You were never abused in any way whatsoever and you know that." I allow him to continue before I answer. "Do you know what that has been like for me? I have lived my whole life by a standard, and now you try to destroy me with those lies? Do you know what that feels like?"

"I know, and I was wrong. I was so wrong in every way. I will never know how badly that hurt you. I will never know the pain it caused but I am sorry, and I will do anything I can to make it right."

"I have some questions you will have to answer for me, Lindsey, and DO NOT lie to me . . ."

"I won't."

"I spent months, years even, telling you I was uncomfortable with you and Tristan. Did you sleep with him?"

"No, I didn't. I promise I did not."

"Did you kiss him? Touch him in any way inappropriate?"

"I did not. Nothing like that at all. We never even held hands. We never hugged in a way that was romantic."

"Did you talk about a life together? Did you hope to be with him if we divorced?"

"I never wanted to be with him romantically. We talked

of having a company and a school together, but we never planned to have a future like a marriage or family together. We never even spoke of things like that." I decide to continue. "I made him my best friend, and the friendship was completely inappropriate. My heart got completely involved. I let him take your place and I was wrong. It might as well have been that we were physical, because the pain it caused you is the same. Whether we were physical or not, I will never speak to him again. The last time I did was months ago, and I promise I never will again. I have blocked him on everything. My phone, all social media, everything. I was wrong. I lied to you about him, about everything surrounding my job, all of it. I'm so sorry."

"Have you had sex with anyone else? Any of the guys you were with?"

Here it is . . . this is the question I have been dreading more than any other. If I tell him the truth I will probably lose any chance I had for reconciliation. I know I will. If I lie I will most certainly lose him. Even if I lied and he never found out, I would still know. God would know. I gave him my word I wouldn't lie, and I will not. He deserves the truth. Oh God, please help me. Please help him.

"Yes. I had sex with one of them."

My heart drops to my feet as soon as the words leave my mouth. Another bullet. It is like I shot him again. He exhales heavily, gets up and stands next to the wall beside him. The sound of his sobbing rips me apart.

"What am I supposed to do with that, Lindsey?"

"I was a whore, Casey." Tears begin to fall down my cheeks again. "I was a whore and I am sorry." I don't know what else to say. I deserve for him to leave. He does not need someone like me. He deserves so much better. He deserves someone faithful to him; someone pure and whole. Suddenly, I realize how much I just want him to be happy, and that it cannot be with me. I would give anything in the world to be with him, but he shouldn't be with me. How desperately I wish I had chosen a different path for my life. How desperately I wish I could be whole for him.

"You have to tell me, Lindsey, I have to know everything," he says through his tears. He keeps his back to me as I tell him everything that happened that dreadful night. He simply listens as I tell him about all the guys I dated through the separation. I tell him everything. I know I have to.

As I finish he comes back to his seat on the couch. We sit in silence for a long time. There is not much that can be said right now. At the same time there are years' worth of things that need to be said.

For the next four hours we dig through the years of pain. Some moments are easy, most are the hardest things I have ever sat through. They are not hard because of what he has said—on the contrary. He is showing me more mercy even in the way he is talking to me than I will ever deserve. Seeing him in so much pain, seeing the one person I love more than anyone on earth hurt, wanting so badly to take all of his pain away and take it all on myself, while knowing the whole time I cannot do that—that is what is so hard. I want to help him and I can't. I want to heal him, and I can't. I want to make it as if none of it ever happened. But it did happen. I can't change any of it. The damage is done.

Can we call a time-out? I want to take my keys and walk out. Even for just a moment to get my breath. Not because I am angry, not at all, but because I cannot keep seeing him this way. How can I even think that? I am a coward to want to leave this talk. A coward! How would I feel if he had done to me what I did to him and then thought, "I need a break, 'cause it's hard"? How is any of this hard for me? I tore him apart, drew his blood, intentionally destroyed as much of him as possible, and he still agreed to talk with me. There is nothing, nothing, nothing that I have the right to walk away from. He might need to do this every day—maybe even every hour if I get the chance to have him again. I will let him do it every day for as long as he needs to if it will prove to him that I am in this for real and in it for the long run.

By two in the morning we have discussed about as much as we can handle for the first conversation. I am hoping beyond hope he will let me come back and talk to him again. I don't care if it is bad or tense. I don't care if he has to dump his load on me every day for the rest of our lives. I love him enough to do it.

"Casey, I will never be able to make up for what I did to you. I have no defenses, no excuses. I was completely and totally wrong, and I know an apology will not make up for any of it. I want to take full ownership for it all. You did nothing to deserve what I did to you. You were a wonderful, loving husband even in the face of me being so cruel to you. If we could make this work, I want you to know that I will give everything up. I don't ever want to dance again—and I mean that with all my heart. I don't ever have to stand on a platform for the rest of my life. I just want you. You are enough for me. I do not need anything else, and I am sorry that I never saw that before. I will stay home and do nothing but love you, love our girls, and love our home, and I will be the happiest, most content woman in the world. I just want you. I want you more than any of it. I will never be able to make up for how I have broken your heart. I cheated on you, heart and body. I cannot take that back and I can't take back the hurt it has caused you. I became the whore, the harlot; I gave myself away knowingly. I sinned against God and you. Even if we don't make it, even if you choose to say no, I ask you to please forgive me. I don't deserve you, and I never will. But please forgive me."

Casey says nothing. He is leaning back in his seat again, arms crossed, looking away, chewing the inside of his cheek. I know the conversation is over for tonight, but I don't feel it would be right to just walk out. So I ask, in total sincerity, "Is there anything else you want to talk about?" Though we are both drained and exhausted, mentally and emotionally, I would still be willing to sit here for the rest of the night, even if we never spoke a word and sat in silence. Finally he speaks.

"Yeah, there is something I want to say."

Here it comes. Oh Lord, please help me. I know I was mentally prepared for him to say "No" to me but now, knowing it is about to leave his lips, is more that I can bear. I want to be with him so badly, and to hear him say "No" will crush me. But I'll still try again tomorrow. God, please, PLEASE, give me the strength to get through this coming moment.

"You're right, Lindsey, this was your fault. I never wanted this. I never wanted to end our marriage. You did this to me. You did this to the girls."

Oh God help me accept his no. Give me strength to hear it. "You are the one who chose this life. I NEVER wanted it. But there is one thing you are NOT right on, Lindsey—you're not a whore. You never have been, no matter what you did."

Did he just . . . maybe I heard him wrong? Maybe I imagined him saying that, but he said it. I cheated on him, I dated multiple guys while we were separated but still married. Of course that's what I was. How can he say otherwise? How can he think otherwise? Surely he is not agreeing to, or even hinting at, a second chance? No. I will not even hope for that, yet. Talking to him has been more than I could have imagined.

All I can do is nod at his statement. I am stunned he said that in the midst of what I have done to him. Knowing that there is nothing else I can say, I stand and go to pick up my keys. When I turn around to say goodbye, and to ask him to meet again, he is standing, too.

"Come here."

Surely not? Oh God, I cannot dare to hope for this.

Casey reaches his arms out, and embraces me. I turn to Jell-O in his arms. I begin weeping. Out of the shame I am living in I cannot hug him back. All I manage is to weep while he holds me. Why is he doing this? I should be holding him and soothing his tears. I should be comforting him, not the other way around. He steps back and lifts my face with his hands.

His eyes . . . Oh, those eyes . . . those dark blue, piercing eyes—usually so full of hurt, but now something different. Forgiveness? Love? Unconditional love.

"I don't want you to leave."

Weeping I reply, "I don't have to leave. I love you so much, Casey."

"I love you. I always have. You're home now, and I love you."

Chapter 28

HOPE IS NEVER LOST

Never in my wildest dreams did I think I would find myself where I am today. I stand in awe of God and His unending kindness and mercy to me. He truly restores beyond what we can think, dream, or imagine. He gives exceedingly, abundantly, and above. At the time of writing, it has been almost two years since my homecoming. Casey and I are fully restored! God did in a moment what would have taken years of counseling. People told me it would be impossible. They said there was so much damage done we would never be able to pick up where we left off and move forward. Others said it would be a miracle if our restoration lasted more than a month or two. They were all wrong. I am more in love with that man than I have ever been in my life, and he loves me with a love I never knew existed. He sees me as God sees me: forgiven.

Our two gorgeous girls, Analeise and Katie, celebrated with us in tears when their Mommy came home. Our family is whole again—completely whole . . . I am whole. We gave Analeise the honor of tearing to pieces the final copy of what was to be our divorce papers. She ripped them to smithereens and laughed as she threw them into the air, as we stood in the living room of that ivy-covered house, our first home. Though they are so young, God heard the pleas of two little girls and answered their every prayer.

My relationship with my mother, sister, brother-in-law, and family is healed, whole, and stronger than it has ever been. We spend countless nights together at Mom's eating, laughing, and loving. They forgave. They forgot. They stood with me through restoration and now we all stand together through life. The Lord did exactly what He said He would do: He answered every call.

December 1st, 2016, Casey and I welcomed our first son Casey Asher Huck Doss into the world. He has my sister's beautiful blonde hair, porcelain skin, and solitary dimple on his left cheek. He has my blue eyes and Casey's strong bone structure and mouth. Every day I look into his face and see the faithfulness of God and the mercy He has shown me. In the faces of my three stunning children are the blessings God pours on me every day, when I did not deserve any of it. He is faithful. His word is true, and He makes good on every promise.

If you find yourself reading this, and you are the one believing for a husband or wife, a son or a daughter, let my story stand as a beacon of hope for you. Let it stand as a reminder that *nothing* is impossible for God. Let it ignite in you a belief for the impossible again, to pray again. I know that what you are going through is the most painful and hardest thing you have ever faced in your life. I know there are no words to adequately describe the anger, hurt, and betrayal that you feel. It takes everything within you to make it through today, much less some unknown amount of time before your miracle shows up at your door. You are angry at the person you love, angry with the people trying to tell you what to do, maybe even angry at God. Everything in you may be screaming to give up, to let them go, and move on. But if I told you they would be home tomorrow, would you give up today?

There is a picture I found once online, an animated picture portraying a diamond miner. He has dug with his pick ax what seems like an endless tunnel, one that must have taken him months. He is weary, covered in dirt, and has just turned around to walk back out of his tunnel, dragging his ax behind him. He has given up. What he does not see is the wall of diamond just beyond the spot he stopped digging. It would have been one strike away. Just one.

Casey and my family believed not for a month, or even six months for me to come home. They believed for over two years. They kept digging in that tunnel.

While I betrayed them, denied them, spat in their face and drew their blood: STRIKE, another dig. When I cheated on Casey, lied about him, made false accusations of him being abusive and cruel: STRIKE, another dig. When I met Casey to pick up the girls with another man in my car: STRIKE. When I moved away to another city: STRIKE. What if they had quit digging just one week before I picked up my phone and emailed Casey?

Little did I know, at the time, exactly one week prior to my "pigpen" moment, my mother was in her car yelling in faith, "Lindsey and Casey are getting back together!" STRIKE! She was picking up her phone, pretending to call people and saying in faith, "Did you hear? Lindsey came home. The girls are thrilled! I have never seen Lindsey and Casey so happy." STRIKE! What if she had quit? She was doing this at the time when things were at their very worst, where there was literally nothing to go on. No hope at all. Nothing but the words she had received from God during the two years. And nothing was going to move her from those words. She didn't know that exactly one week to the day I would be knocking on her door asking her to forgive me, to take me back in, to help me and pray with me to restore my marriage to Casey. She didn't know that last strike in the tunnel was going to be the one that broke through that last layer of dirt.

What if Casey had moved on while we were still separated? After all, I had moved on. What if he had done the same? What if he had given up and allowed the pain of what I did to him push him to another woman? It's not that he didn't have the opportunity. He did. He had several women chomping at the bit for him to give them even one passing glance, and although he was the one wronged, not for one moment, not in thought or in deed, did he ever give in. He believed, he fought, he prayed, and his miracle showed up.

You never know which day will be your tomorrow. Your tomorrow may be in a day, in a week, or it may not happen for another two or more years. Do you want it enough to keep fighting for it? Do you want the marriage enough to stay faithful, even when your spouse did not? Do you want your son or daughter to come home badly enough that you'll keep fighting for and loving them, even when it hurts? After all, right this very second may be your day before tomorrow.

If, on the other hand, you are the one reading this book and living at a crossroad in your own life, I implore you: make the right choice. Make the choice that is backed by the Word and the will of God—even if it is not what *you* want at the moment. The Word and will of the Lord will always return back to you with great reward, but the choice of deception will bring with it a curse. When you willingly and knowingly walk away from the will and purpose of God, choosing sin, you will be given over to face the consequences of those choices alone.

Can you be forgiven? Of course! But the price you pay

will be high. When you are walking in relationship with God and walking in truth you will face life's trials with the hand of God's grace upon you. I know the life you see in front of you looks like the easier road, a far more rewarding choice, but it will leave an emptiness inside you, a void you will never be able to fill. The enemy will only show you a mirage of the life he is offering. He will never reveal the real price you will have to pay.

What this book could not hold are the countless consequences I faced, and am still facing, as a result of my choices. The people involved in my story are facing consequences too, as a result of the choices they made through my influence. It's not that I didn't have any warning—on the contrary, I had warning after warning after warning. But I made a choice to ignore those warnings, I made the choice to cover them up, to blame someone else for my actions, or twist the Word of God so that I could make it apply to decisions I knew were wrong. If you read this and have to ask yourself if what you're doing is wrong, it probably is. When you know you walk in truth, there is no doubt. There is perfect peace, and no matter how many excuses you have for the actions and choices you are making, at the end of the day, in the deepest part of your heart, you know which choice is right.

You may think you are too far-gone—you're not. You may have even journeyed further than I did—it's still not too far for the love of Christ. You may have even completely lost a marriage, or two or three. Your spouse may have moved on and remarried and now you are left with no hope of restoring anything. Or, you might have been the one who left, moved on and married another. It does not mean the second marriage need be torn apart. It does not. It still does not mean God does not have a plan for you. He does, and what a glorious and beautiful plan it is! God's glorious plan for you follows repentance. It matters not how far you are or how far you have gone. Repentance is a matter of the heart—it is seeing ourselves in true light; it is taking ownership for everything we have done and truly making a radical change to never do it again; it is repenting without an excuse, and without a defense. You cannot change what you do not acknowledge, what you do not take extreme ownership for—but, if you really do want to change, if you really do want to re-route the course of your future and change your fate, then acknowledgement is your first step, and a resolve to never make the same mistake again is your second.

If you are the one who is most like me in the story, take a good, hard, long look at your life and ask yourself if you are, or are not, on the right path. Take note of the pricks the Spirit has been giving you. Take note of the red flags God is waving at you, warning you to stop and turn around. Take an honest look in the mirror and ask God if it is you who needs to change. It is so easy—frighteningly easy—to believe you are walking in truth when you are actually walking in deception; to go to church and prayer meetings, to be a leader or even a pastor's wife or pastor, and be far away from where you're supposed to be. Before you know what's happening, your music changes, your friends change, your movies, clothes, hair, who you are dressing up for, everything changes. Turn around before you find yourself down a path that you cannot come back from.

If you have found yourself in this place, in desperate need of restoration, of hope, trust me when I say, it is available for you. It is waiting for you. God really is there with open arms; He really is willing to give you another chance, but you have to be all in.

The path to restoration is not an easy one—and let no one tell you it is. It takes hard work. It is extremely difficult to look in the mirror, truly face yourself and the consequences of your choices, take ownership for them and actually change them. It seems humiliating to think you will have to stand in front of everyone and own up for what you did, all the people you may have lied to or hurt, all the people who are believing and praying for you: your husband, wife, mother, father, sisters, brothers, friends, children, pastors, church congregation, everyone. But those people are the ones who really love you, the ones who will forgive you and help you walk out your restoration process.

Most people see the highlight reel of restoration: the restored marriage, holding hands as you walk down the sidewalk, the daughter or son back home laughing and eating dinner with their family. What they do not see is the commitment it takes for all people involved, but especially the one who ran away. They do not see the resolve it takes to set your mind to forever change and never look back; to be willing to do anything, give up anything, anyone even, to be right with God; to not care how long it takes to repair things, to build trust back up. They don't see the tears, the hours upon hours of digging through the mire. Are you willing to try? Are you willing to give truth and love another shot?

CONCLUSION

Divorce. Separation. Believing, with no hope, for another that we love. These things we face in life are never easy, and the easy road is rarely the one that keeps us in obedience to God. If it were, it wouldn't be hard. Obedience is hard because it is almost never what we want to do. Admitting our wrongs, going back to our spouse, making amends with our broken families, facing the fear, putting aside our feelings, and choosing truth, even when it is not what we want; maybe even having to at least apologize to God and to the spouse who has already moved on and married another. Though a marriage restoration would not be available there, it doesn't mean there isn't hope for true love and a blessed and wonderful future for you, and it doesn't mean clearing up offenses and bitterness is impossible. Find hope in this story of my friend Dianna. Like me her decisions cost her everything; her home, her marriage, and her career. As time passed, her divorce became final, and her husband moved on with into a new marriage. When Dianna realized the truth of her life choices, going back to her first marriage was not an option, but going home was. Ultimately for all of us, home is found in the presence of our Heavenly Father. Returning to God Dianne found healing, wholeness and restoration of her identity as a daughter of God; but God not only heals, he blesses far beyond. The Lord recently blessed her with an incredible man of God. She is now happily married and has begun a brand new journey. While circumstances for each of us may be different, and the journey to each destiny unique, home is the same for everyone. It is with our Father. There we ultimately find our healing, restoration, and identity.

It is when we choose to obey even when it means taking the path less traveled that our lives take a turn for the better: truth, hope, love, faith, and joy. It is when we choose God and His will, no matter what it looks like or what it costs us, that we become truly free.

Is the road to restoration hard? Yes it is, but the road of sin is harder. Is sin worth it? No, but restoration definitely is. Maybe you are asking yourself, "How do I get home?" Well, you probably know exactly the direction in which your first step needs to be.

So go ahead. Take the leap.

I dare you.

"So he returned home to his father. And while he was still a long way off, his father saw him coming. Filled with love and compassion, he ran to his son, embraced him, and kissed him. His son said to him, 'Father, I have sinned against both heaven and you, and I am no longer worthy of being called your son.' But his father said to the servants, 'Quick! Bring the finest robe in the house and put it on him. Get a ring for his finger and sandals for his feet. And kill the calf we have been fattening. We must celebrate with a feast, for this son of mine was dead and has now returned to life. He was lost, but now he is found.'"

Luke 15:20-24

Final Letter

I may never have the opportunity to face or speak to the people who were part of my two-year journey. So, to those of you who have happened to pick up this book, those who joined me in my journey, please accept my most sincere apology. Though I could try to cast the blame on you for aiding in my deception, it was really I who deceived you. I gave you the bitter cup of my own offense. I was wrong. I lied to all of you, and I am truly sorry. I told you my marriage was bad. It was not. I told you Casey was abusive and a tyrant. He was not. I painted a picture of a wounded, sad, hurting woman. It was a mask. I wanted out of the marriage for my own selfish and foolish reasons. Forgive me for any hurt I have caused you and for all the deceptions I caused you to believe.

I repent to you for all of it,

Lindsey

ABOUT THE AUTHOR

Lindsey Doss has served in the ministry her entire life. She and her husband Casey held leadership positions at The Ramp for over fifteen years and are now the Lead Pastors of Hope Unlimited Church in Knoxville, TN. They have three beautiful children: Analeise, Katie and Asher.

You can follow Lindsey on Twitter and Instagram: @lindsey_doss, and on Facebook: Lindsey Doss.

You can also find out more about Casey and Lindsey's ministry at caseydoss.com and hopeunlimited.church.

PRAYER

We hope you enjoyed this book and that it has been both a blessing and a challenge to your life and walk with God. Maybe you just got hold of it and are glancing through before starting. We made the decision as a publishing company right from the start never to take for granted that everyone has prayed a prayer to receive Jesus as their Lord, so we are including that as the finale to this book. If you have never asked Jesus into your life and would like to do that now, it's so easy. Just pray this simple prayer:

Dear Lord Jesus,
Thank You for dying on the cross for me. I believe that You gave Your life so that I could have life. When You died on the cross, You died as an innocent man who had done nothing wrong. You were paying for my sins and the debt I could never pay. I believe in You, Jesus, and receive the brand new life and fresh start that the Bible promises that I can have. Thank You for my sins forgiven, for the righteousness that

*comes to me as a gift from You, for hope and love
beyond what I have known and the assurance of
eternal life that is now mine.
Amen.*

Good next moves are to get yourself a Bible that is easy to understand and begin to read. Maybe start in John so you can discover all about Jesus for yourself. Start to pray—prayer is simply talking to God—and, finally, find a church that's alive and get your life planted in it. These simple ingredients will cause your relationship with God to grow.

Why not email us and let us know if you did that so we can rejoice with you?

The Great Big Life Publishing team
info@greatbiglifepublishing.com

FURTHER INFORMATION

For further information about the author of this book, or to order more copies, please contact:

Great Big Life Publishing
Empower Centre
83-87 Kingston Road
Portsmouth
Hampshire
PO2 7DX
United Kingdom
info@greatbiglifepublishing.com

Or visit our website: http://greatbiglifepublishing.com.

ARE YOU AN AUTHOR?

Do you have a word from God on your heart that you're looking to get published to a wider audience? We're looking for manuscripts that identify with our own vision of bringing life-giving and relevant messages to Body of Christ. Send yours for review towards possible publication to:

Great Big Life Publishing
Empower Centre
83-87 Kingston Road
Portsmouth
Hampshire
PO2 7DX
United Kingdom
info@greatbiglifepublishing.com